Two Faces of Liberalism

TWO FACES OF LIBERALISM

JOHN GRAY

The New Press

First published in the United Kingdom by Polity Press in
association with Blackwell Publishers Ltd, 2000
Published in the United States by The New Press, New York, 2000
Distributed by W. W. Norton & Company, Inc., New York

LIBRARY OF CONGRESS CATALOGING-IN-PUBLICATION DATA
Gray, John, 1948–
Two faces of liberalism / John Gray.
p. cm.
Includes bibliographical references and index.
ISBN 1-56584-589-7 (hc.)
1. Liberalism. I. Title.
JC574.G73 2000
320.51—dc21   00–037238

The New Press was established in 1990 as a not-for-profit alternative
to the large, commercial publishing houses currently dominating
the book publishing industry. The New Press operates in the public
interest rather than for private gain, and is committed to publishing,
in innovative ways, works of educational, cultural, and community
value that are often deemed insufficiently profitable.

The New Press, 450 West 41ˢᵗ Street, 6ᵗʰ floor, New York, NY 10036
www.thenewpress.com

Set in 11/13 pt. Berling
Printed in the United States of America

10 9 8 7 6 5 4 3 2 1

Contents

Acknowledgements

A good many debts have been incurred writing this short book. Conversations over many years with Isaiah Berlin and Michael Oakeshott helped shape some of the ideas that it contains. Conversations with Joseph Raz and Raymond Plant have also been formative.

A seminar led by Yehuda Elkana and Wolf Lepenies during a visit to the Wissenshaftskolleg in Berlin enabled me to formulate my thoughts more clearly on a number of questions. John Burrow, Geoffrey Smith and Charles Spinosa gave valuable comments on an early draft. Exchanges with Steve Erikson, Henry Hardy and Jonathan Riley were also helpful.

In all these cases, all the usual caveats apply.

My greatest debt is to Mieko, to whom I dedicate this book.

JOHN GRAY

Two Faces of Liberalism

1

Liberal Toleration

The liberal state originated in a search for *modus vivendi*. Contemporary liberal regimes are late flowerings of a project of toleration that began in Europe in the sixteenth century. The task we inherit is refashioning liberal toleration so that it can guide the pursuit of *modus vivendi* in a more plural world.

Liberal toleration has contributed immeasurably to human well-being. Nowhere so deep-rooted that it can be taken for granted, it is an achievement that cannot be valued too highly. We cannot do without that early modern ideal; but it cannot be our guide in late modern circumstances. For the ideal of toleration we have inherited embodies two incompatible philosophies. Viewed from one side, liberal toleration is the ideal of a rational consensus on the best way of life. From the other, it is the belief that human beings can flourish in many ways of life.

If liberalism has a future, it is in giving up the search for a rational consensus on the best way of life. As a consequence of mass migration, new technologies of communication and continued cultural experimentation, nearly all societies today contain several ways of life, with many people belonging to more than one. The liberal ideal of toleration which looks to a rational consensus on the best way of life was born in societies divided on the claims of a single way of life. It cannot show us how to live together in societies that harbour many ways of life.

Toleration did not begin with liberalism. In ancient Alexandria and Buddhist India, among the Romans, the Moors and the Ottomans, different faiths coexisted in peace for long periods. Yet the ideal of a common life that does not rest on common beliefs is a liberal inheritance. Our task is to consider what becomes of this patrimony in societies which are much more deeply diverse than those in which liberal toleration was conceived.

Liberalism has always had two faces. From one side, toleration is the pursuit of an ideal form of life. From the other, it is the search for terms of peace among different ways of life. In the former view, liberal institutions are seen as applications of universal principles. In the latter, they are a means to peaceful coexistence. In the first, liberalism is a prescription for a universal regime. In the second, it is a project of coexistence that can be pursued in many regimes.

The philosophies of John Locke and Immanuel Kant exemplify the liberal project of a universal regime, while those of Thomas Hobbes and David Hume express the liberalism of peaceful coexistence. In more recent times, John Rawls and F.A. Hayek have defended the first liberal philosophy, while Isaiah Berlin and Michael Oakeshott are exemplars of the second.

The ideal of toleration as a means to truth was stated canonically by Locke. In Locke's account, liberal toleration was far from being sceptical about truth in religion or morality. It presupposed that truth had been found, and imposed a duty on government to promote it. It was toleration of things that were judged to be bad or false.[1]

Locke understood toleration as a pathway to the one true religion. He did not extend toleration to Catholics or atheists, if only because he was not confident that persuasion would lead them to that faith. Locke's defence of toleration was that it enables us to discover the best life for humankind. He never doubted that there was such a thing. Throughout its history, the liberal ideal of toleration as a means to a universal rational consensus has rested on the same conviction.

Yet from the beginnings of liberal thought there was another understanding of toleration. Nothing in Hobbes suggests he favoured toleration as a pathway to the true faith.
For him, toleration was a strategy of peace. Indifferent to belief, the sole concern of government was with practice. In this
Hobbesian view, the end of toleration is not consensus. It is
coexistence.[2]

For liberal thinkers who sought a rational consensus on the
best life, toleration was a remedy for the limitations of human
understanding. As Voltaire put it: 'What is toleration? It is
the appurtenance of humanity. We are all full of weakness
and errors; let us mutually pardon each other for our follies.'[3]
Liberal thinkers have never been over-sanguine about the pros-
pects of people reaching agreement in their beliefs about the
good life. They have always been too conscious of the force of
the passions to view reason as anything more than a frail power
in human affairs.

It was this manifest imperfection of human reason that underpinned the ideal of toleration as a means to consensus. The
hope of a rational consensus on values supports the liberal
philosophies that prevail today. Yet the idea that the persistence of many ways of life is a mark of imperfection has little
to support it.

Rational inquiry in ethics does not yield consensus on the
best life. It shows that the good life comes in many varieties.
The idea that the exercise of reason produces agreement is at
least as old as Plato's Socrates. Even so, there has never been
much to support it. Reason can enlighten us as to our ethical
conflicts. Often, it shows them to be deeper than we thought,
and leaves us in the lurch as to how to resolve them.

Liberal regimes are often viewed as solutions to a modern
problem of pluralism. Yet what is most notable about the early
modern societies from which liberal regimes emerged is how
homogeneous they were. Few, if any, late modern societies
display as much consensus in their values and beliefs. It is not
only that they differ greatly from one another. Most of them
contain several ways of life, honouring different goods and
virtues.

The fact that society contains different forms of ethical life is far from being peculiarly modern. On the contrary, in their diversity of ways of life late modern societies have something in common with the ancient world. What is new in the modern world is not acceptance of diversity in styles of life. It is hostility to hierarchies.

The cultures from which European moral philosophy emerged contained many forms of ethical life. Greek polytheism expressed the belief that the sources of value are irreducibly plural. If it recognized the idea of the best human life, it was one in which many distinct and at times conflicting sources of value were honoured. In their acceptance of many sources of value, the Greeks were at one with other ancient cultures: ancient Judaism imposed few universal obligations; Hinduism recognized different duties in different stations and stages of life.

Ancient societies were more hospitable to differences than ours. This is partly because the idea of human equality was weak or absent. Modernity begins not with the recognition of difference but with a demand for uniformity. There is nothing new in the idea that the good life may vary with different people. To think that it is distinctively modern is a mere prejudice.

Ancient pluralism found few echoes in Greek philosophy. The founders of European ethical theory were monists. Neither Plato nor Aristotle was in any doubt that one way of life was best for humankind. Whether the good for humans was finally one, as Plato imagined, or many, as Aristotle was sometimes ready to admit, the best kind of life was the same for everyone – even though they never doubted that it could be lived fully only by a few leisured Greek males. In this classical view, conflicting judgements about the human good are symptoms of error. For the founders of European ethical theory, as for the Christians who came after them, conflicts of value were signs of imperfection, not a normal part of ethical life.

From its beginnings, moral philosophy has been a struggle to exorcize conflict from ethical life. The same is true of political thought. European political philosophy has been deeply marked by the resistance to conflict that shaped Greek ethics. In the city, as in the soul, harmony has been the ideal. Most liberal thinkers have taken over the Socratic, Christian and Enlightenment faith in the harmony of values. But an ideal of harmony is not the best starting-point for thinking about ethics or government. It is better to begin by understanding why conflict – in the city as in the soul – cannot be avoided.

In the form that we have inherited it, liberal toleration is an ideal of rational consensus. As heirs to that project, we need an ideal based not on a rational consensus on the best way of life, nor on reasonable disagreement about it, but instead on the truth that humans will always have reason to live differently. *Modus vivendi* is such an ideal. It embodies an older current of liberal thought about toleration, and applies it to our own new circumstances.

Modus vivendi expresses the belief that there are many forms of life in which humans can thrive. Among these there are some whose worth cannot be compared. Where such ways of life are rivals, there is no one of them that is best. People who belong to different ways of life need have no disagreement. They may simply be different.

Whereas our inherited conception of toleration presupposes that one way of life is best for all of humankind, *modus vivendi* accepts that there are many forms of life, some of them no doubt yet to be contrived, in which humans can flourish. For the predominant ideal of liberal toleration, the best life may be unattainable, but it is the same for all. From a standpoint of *modus vivendi*, no kind of life can be the best for everyone. The human good is too diverse to be realized in any life. Our inherited ideal of toleration accepts with regret the fact that there are many ways of life. If we adopt *modus vivendi* as our ideal we will welcome it.

Ethical inquiry does not yield a single way of life or scheme of values for all – not even for a single individual. Instead it shows that people have reason to live in different ways. Different ways of life embody incompatible aspects of the human good. So, in different contexts, may a single human life. Yet no life can reconcile fully the rival values that the human good contains.

The aim of *modus vivendi* cannot be to still the conflict of values. It is to reconcile individuals and ways of life honouring conflicting values to a life in common. We do not need common values in order to live together in peace. We need common institutions in which many forms of life can coexist.

The span of good lives of which humans are capable cannot be contained in any one community or tradition. The good for humans is too beset by conflict for that to be possible. For the same reason, the good life cannot be contained in any one political regime. A theory of *modus vivendi* is not the search for an ideal regime, liberal or otherwise. It has no truck with the notion of an ideal regime. It aims to find terms on which different ways of life can live well together.

Modus vivendi is liberal toleration adapted to the historical fact of pluralism. The ethical theory underpinning *modus vivendi* is value-pluralism. The most fundamental value-pluralist claim is that there are many conflicting kinds of human flourishing, some of which cannot be compared in value. Among the many kinds of good lives that humans can live there are some that are neither better nor worse than one another, nor the same in worth, but incommensurably – that is to say, differently – valuable. Even so, there may be good reasons for preferring some incommensurable goods over others.

Value-pluralism is closer to ethical theories which affirm the possibility of moral knowledge than it is to familiar kinds of ethical scepticism, subjectivism or relativism. It enables us to reject some judgements about the good as being in error. At the same time, it means giving up a traditional notion of truth in ethics. To affirm that the good is plural is to allow that it harbours conflicts for which there is no one solution that is right. It is not that there can be no right solution in such conflicts. Rather, there are many.

The good is independent of our perspectives on it, but it is not the same for all. It is not just that different ways of life honour different goods and virtues. More, what one way of life praises another condemns. Value-pluralism is the claim that both may be right. This claim is paradoxical. It seems to imply a tolerance of contradiction that classical logic prohibits. There is paradox here, but not – or so I shall argue – of the kind that should concern us. It may be that the good cannot contain contradictions; but it shows itself in ways of life that are incompatible.

Conflicts of value need not express any uncertainty, practical or intellectual, about what is good. At their starkest, they exclude any such uncertainty. They are conflicts within the good itself. However variously they may be understood, peace and justice are universal goods; but sometimes they make demands that are incompatible. When peace and justice are rivals, which is worse, war or injustice? Neither has automatic or universal priority. Peace may be more urgent than justice; the claims of justice may override the immediate needs of peace. In conflicts of this kind, people need not differ about the content of the good or the right. Where they differ is on how their rival claims are to be reconciled.

Justice does not speak always with one voice. The communities that are locked in conflict in Israel and Ulster may claim that they invoke the same principles of justice. Yet their judgements of what is just and what unjust in the context of their contemporary conflicts are deeply at odds. In part, this reflects their different interpretations of their shared history. Partly, no doubt, it is also an expression of the fact that their interests are in many ways opposed. When communities contend for power over scarce resources, they are likely to seek to justify their rival interests by arguments of fairness. Where interests are at odds and political power is at stake, shared principles of justice are likely to yield incompatible judgements of what justice demands.

But conflicts over what justice demands do not come only from these familiar facts. Justice itself makes incompatible demands. When justice requires that restitution be made for injustice done to communities in the past, the result may be unjust to present generations. A claim for the return of land that was unjustly expropriated may collide with a no less just claim to the land that is based on generations of working it. Such conflicts do not arise from an imperfect sense of justice. They express the truth that justice itself encompasses conflicting values.

Even if a conception of justice could be formulated that received universal assent, it would make conflicting demands about which reasonable people could differ. Once again, this is not because human reason is imperfect. It is because incompatible solutions of such conflicts can be equally reasonable.

That conflicts between universal values can be settled in incompatible ways is one reason why people belong to different ways of life. The many ways in which humans can live well embody different settlements among discordant universal values. Contrary to the liberal ideal of toleration, the fact of divergent ways of life is not a result of the frailty of reason. It embodies the truth that humans have reason to live differently.

At the same time, some conflicts of value do arise from rival views of the good. They come not from rivalry among values that are universal but from the different goods that are honoured in particular ways of life. Some goods that are central in some ways of life are absent, or else marginal, in others. In late modern societies, personal autonomy and romantic love are highly valued; but these rival goods are far from being valued by everyone. Today, as in the past, there are ways of life that do not celebrate them, or which condemn them.

To be caught between the demands of different ways of life is a common source of moral conflict. Many people face conflicts among values for which there is no single right solution. The fact that ways of life honour different goods and virtues is not a mark of imperfection. It is a sign that humans can live well in different ways.

Yet not all ways of life allow humans to live well. There are universal human goods and evils. Some virtues are needed for any kind of human flourishing. Without courage and prudence no life can go well. Without sympathy for the suffering and happiness of others, the artefact of justice cannot be maintained. Forms of life that are deficient in these virtues are lacking in the conditions of human well-being. Such values are generically human. Because they are universal they can be used to assess any particular way of life.

That some values are incommensurable does not mean that all ways of life have the same value. The bottom line for value-pluralism is the diversity of goods and evils, not of ways of life. Different ways of life can be more or less successful in achieving universal goods, mitigating universal evils and in resolving conflicts among them.

Even so, universal values do not fit together to compose an ideal life – for the species, for particular societies or for individuals. Rather, if universal values can be rivals, there can be no such thing as an ideal life. There may be a best life for any individual; but not one that is without loss. In particular ways of life there may be better or worse solutions to conflicts of value, but none that meets fully every legitimate claim. There are better and worse regimes, and some that are thoroughly illegitimate; but none that fully realizes all universal values, and is thereby a model for all the rest.

The most fundamental differences amongst ways of life arise from the manner in which they deal with conflicts among values that are universal. Universal values enable us to assess particular ways of life; but they do not add up to a universal morality.

In the world as we find it, even the barest requirements of a life worth living cannot all be always met in full. Toppling a tyranny may trigger civil war. Protecting a broad range of liberal freedoms may result in the regime that guarantees them being short-lived. At the same time, supporting a strong state as a bulwark against anarchy may worsen the abuse of power. Wise policy can temper these conflicts. It cannot hope to overcome them.

Conflicts of value go with being human. The reason is not that human beings have rival beliefs about the good life. Nor is it – though this comes closer to the nub of the matter – that the right action sometimes has wrong as its shadow. It is that human needs make conflicting demands. The idea of a human life that is without conflicts of value runs aground on the contradictions of human needs.

It is not only that, because they make incompatible demands on scarce material resources, human needs may be practically at odds. More, they can be met fully only in forms of life that cannot be combined. The lives of a professional soldier and a carer in a leprosarium, of a day trader on the stock market and a contemplative in a monastery, cannot be mixed without loss.

Such lives embody virtues that do not easily coexist; and they may express beliefs that are contradictory. Yet each answers to a human need.

The best human lives are very different from one another, and often incompatible. This is not a truth of logic. It is a fact about human nature. As such it is not unalterable. Perhaps, as technologies of genetic engineering advance, human beings will be tempted to alter the biological endowments that have enabled them to live in so many different ways. There is nothing to say such attempts cannot succeed; but if they do they will destroy much that has hitherto been of value in human life.

Conflicts of value come from the competing needs of our common human nature. A kind of moral scarcity is built into the fabric of human life. It is because human needs are contradictory that no human life can be perfect. That does not mean that human life is imperfect. It means that the idea of perfection has no meaning. The idea of conflicting and incommensurable values is far from the Augustinian notion that all things human are imperfect. Augustine contrasted the imperfection of the human world with the perfection of the divine. By contrast, rivalry between incommensurable values destroys the very idea of perfection.

The fact that good harbours conflicts of value does not mean that the human condition must always be tragic. To be sure, tragic choices cannot be eliminated from ethical life. Where universal values make conflicting demands, the right action may contain wrong. When values clash in this way, there may be irreparable loss. Then there is surely tragedy.

But the plurality of values signifies more than simply tragedy. It means that there are many kinds of life in which humans can thrive. Where these lives are so different from one another that their worth cannot be compared, it makes little sense to speak of gain or loss. When such lives cannot be combined, they need not be antagonists; they may be alternatives. If we choose among them, as sometimes we must, the choice need not be tragic. It may simply bespeak the abundance of flourishing lives that is open to us.

If this is true, it has always been so. Value-pluralism is an account of ethical life, not an intepretation of pluralism in late modern societies. If it is true, it is a truth about human nature, not the contemporary condition. Nevertheless, value-pluralism has a special application to late modern societies.

In nearly all contemporary societies the coexistence of many ways of life is an established fact. Though distinct, these ways of life are not independent. They interact continuously – so much so that it may be hard to tell the difference between them. Indeed, since many people belong to more than one, it may be impossible to distinguish them completely. Ways of life are tricky things to get to know. They do not come ready labelled. There is no sure-fire method of enumerating them. And they come in many varieties.

There is the way of life of religious fundamentalists and secular liberals, of countryfolk and 'young urban profession-als', of Taliban and Quakers, of first-generation immigrants and that of their children, of Homer's warrior-class, the Desert Fathers and twenty-first-century Hasids, and indefinitely many more. It is impossible to specify the necessary and sufficient conditions that must be met for a style of human activity to qualify as a way of life. Nor is it necessary. We can distinguish them by a loose bundle of criteria.

Ways of life must be practised by a number of people, not only one, span the generations, have a sense of themselves and be recognized by others, exclude some people and have some distinctive practices, beliefs and values, and so forth. Often these criteria do not yield a clear result. Two commu-nities may honour many of the same values but be locked in an historical conflict. We might say of them that they have the same way of life but are divided in their allegiances to the regime under which they live. (Think of Ulster.) Or two com-munities may have distinctive and opposed beliefs about the historical sources of their present conflicts, contrasting atti-tudes to a number of social issues, and a strong propensity to exclude one another (by avoiding intermarriage, for exam-ple). Then we might be inclined to say they have conflicting ways of life. (Think again of Ulster.) What counts as a way of life may not always be decidable.

When the standard types of contemporary liberal thought

refer to pluralism they mean the diversity of personal ethical beliefs and ideals. That is not the kind of pluralism that should most concern political philosophy. Late modern societies are notable for the diversity of ways of life they contain. Immigration and the partial erosion of the cohesive national cultures that were constructed earlier in the modern period have increased the number of ethnic and cultural traditions that coexist in the same societies. At the same time, continuing cultural experimentation has produced a number of new styles of life. *This* fact of pluralism was not foreseen in liberal thought. Even now it has not been fully comprehended.

The conflicts of value that rightly shape the agenda of political thought come not from the divergent ideals of individuals but from the rival claims of ways of life. Recent liberal orthodoxy passes over these conflicts because it takes for granted that one way of life is dominant in society. In contrast, value-pluralism has particular relevance to late modern societies in which, by choice, chance or fate, many ways of life have come to coexist.

Liberal thought needs revision if the ideal of toleration is to be refashioned to suit this circumstance. In standard liberal accounts, pluralism refers to a diversity of personal ideals. Liberal thought rarely addresses the deeper diversity that comes when there are different ways of life in the same society and even in the lives of the same individual. Yet it is this latter sort of pluralism that should set the agenda of thought about ethics and government today.

To think of this condition as a peculiar disability of modern times is mistaken.[4] The pot-pourri sometimes called western civilization has always contained conflicting values. Greek, Roman, Christian and Jewish traditions each contain distinctive goods and virtues that cannot be translated fully into the ethical life of the others. The notion of a 'western tradition' in which these irreconcilable elements were once fused cannot withstand philosophical – or historical – scrutiny. There was never a coherent synthesis of these values, nor could there have been. Still, for many centuries, these diverse inheritances were subordinated in European societies to a single ethical ideal. With all its doctrinal variations, and the many prudent allowances it made for the intractability of human nature, the Christian ideal of life succeeded in subjugating or marginalizing others that had been part of the European inheritance for centuries or millennia. Liberalism needs to be rethought to fit a context in which different ideals of life coexist in the same societies – and often the same individuals.

In recent liberal writings, the fact of pluralism refers to a diversity of personal ideals whose place is in the realm of voluntary association. The background idea here is that of the autonomous individual selecting a particular style of life. This type of diversity resembles the diversity of ethnic cuisines that can be found in some cities. Like the choice of an ethnic restaurant, the adoption of a personal ideal occurs in private life. But the fact of pluralism is not the trivial and banal truth that individuals hold to different personal ideals. It is the coexistence of different ways of life. Conventional liberal thought contrives to misunderstand this fact, because it takes for granted a consensus on liberal values.

In reality, though there is unprecedented lip-service to them, most late modern societies contain little consensus on liberal values. Many people belong at once in a liberal form of life and in communities which do not honour liberal values. At the same time, many who stand chiefly in liberal ethical life do not subscribe to some of its traditional values. The liberal ideal of personal autonomy is the idea of being part-author of one's life. For some, the pursuit of autonomy comes into conflict with allegiance to an established community. For others, it is in tension with the freedom to respond to the needs of the present. For all these kinds of people, 'traditional', 'liberal' and 'postmodern', ethical life is inescapably hybrid.

Most late modern societies are far from exhibiting an overlapping consensus on liberal values. Rather, the liberal discourse of rights and personal autonomy is deployed in a continuing conflict to gain and hold power by communities and ways of life having highly diverse values. Where it exists, the hegemony of liberal discourse is often skin-deep.

If it can be found anywhere, an overlapping consensus on liberal values should exist in the United States. And it is true that in the USA there is virtually no group that does not invoke liberal principles. Yet America is no different from the rest of the world in being riven by conflicts between ways of life. The quarter of the American population that espouses creationism, 'the right to life' and other fundamentalist causes does not repudiate liberal values explicitly – as people with similar beliefs might do elsewhere in the world. It appropriates them for its own purposes. The strategic deployment of liberal discourse for fundamentalist ends by a large segment of the population is not a consensus on liberal values. It is practically the opposite. Like other late modern societies, the United States is not hegemonically liberal but morally pluralist.

Recent liberal thinkers claim that the appropriate response to the fact of pluralism is a 'theory of justice'. The 'political liberalism' of John Rawls and his followers claims to advance an account of justice that can be accepted by people who have different conceptions of the good. According to this recent orthodoxy, the liberal state is not just one among a number of regimes that can be legitimate. It is the only mode of political organization that can ever be fully legitimate. In recent liberal thought this claim is conjoined with another – that what makes a liberal state legitimate is its protection of human rights.

For Rawls, as for Ronald Dworkin, F.A. Hayek and Robert Nozick, political philosophy is a branch of the philosophy of law – the branch which concerns justice and fundamental rights. The goal of political philosophy is an ideal constitution, in principle universally applicable, which specifies a fixed framework of basic liberties and human rights. This framework sets the terms – the only terms – on which different ways of life may coexist.

These thinkers claim that conflicts among goods and ways of life can be resolved by reading off the requirements of justice or rights. But the requirements of justice and rights can and do conflict. It is not just that the demands of one right may clash with those of another. A single right may make incompatible demands. There is no uniquely rational way of resolving these conflicts. This truth has large consequences. It means that there can be no such thing as an ideally liberal regime. Because rights make conflicting demands that can reasonably be resolved in different ways, the very idea of such a regime is a mistake.

To say that there cannot be an ideal political regime is not to mount a defence of imperfection in politics. It is to reject the idea of an ideal regime. Different regimes can rightly resolve conflicts among vital human rights in different ways. Some such settlements are better than others, but there is nothing which says that the best regimes will resolve conflicts among rights in similar ways.

On the contrary, because their circumstances and histories vary so much, the best regimes are very different from one another. (So are the worst.) Politics abounds in tragic choices. Even so, it is not because of the tragedies of politics that the idea of an ideal regime lacks sense. It is because the best regimes come in many varieties.

When we differ deeply as to the content of the good, an appeal to rights will not help us. For in that case we will differ as to which rights we have. Fundamental differences about rights express rival conceptions of the good. When rational inquiry leaves our views of the good deeply at odds, it is vain to appeal to rights. Basic human rights can be justified as giving protection against universal human evils; but even such rights clash with one another, and incompatible settlements of their conflicts can be equally legitimate. When universal evils clash, no theory of rights can tell us what to do.

It is the same with social justice. We cannot avoid judgements of fairness regarding the distribution of goods in society. The notion that fairness in procedures is all that society needs in the way of a shared conception of justice, which Hayek made familiar,[5] has little to be said for it. Yet no contemporary society contains a consensus on fairness that is deep or wide enough to ground a 'theory of justice'.

There is no more consensus on what justice means than there is on the character of the good. If anything, there is less. Amongst the virtues, justice is one of the most shaped by convention. For that reason it is among the most changeable. When many ways of life share the same society, it is natural that the sense of justice should vary. It is therefore hardly surprising that liberal philosophers differ about the most fundamental requirements of justice. Today, most liberal thinkers affirm that justice is the supreme virtue of social institutions; but some declare that it demands equal distribution of social goods, others that it requires respect for the supposed fact that each of us owns his or her natural endowments, yet others that it involves matching resources with basic needs or merits – and still others that it has nothing to do with distribution at all. Such differences are to be expected. They mirror differences in moral outlook in the wider society. What is surprising is that they are not seen as an objection to the enterprise that most contemporary liberal thinkers have in common – the attempt to construct a theory of justice. When recent liberal thinkers claim that liberalism is a strictly political doctrine, they mean that it does not depend on any comprehensive conception of the good. They never tire of telling us that the demands of justice must take priority over any ideal of the good. They appear to have overlooked the fact that different views of the good support different views of justice.

Only this oversight can account for the fact that in 'political liberalism' nothing of importance is left to political decision. The basic liberties and the distribution of social goods are matters of justice, and in political liberalism what justice demands is a matter not for political decision but for legal adjudication. The central institution of Rawls's 'political liberalism' is not a deliberative assembly such as a parliament. It is a court of law. All fundamental issues are removed from political deliberation in order to be adjudicated by a Supreme Court. The self-description of Rawlsian doctrine as political liberalism is supremely ironic. In fact, Rawls's doctrine is a species of anti-political legalism.[6]

Liberal legalists differ about the rights we have. Egalitarian legalists, such as Rawls and Dworkin, think we have welfare rights to resources, whereas libertarian legalists such as Nozick and Hayek insist that the only human rights are rights against aggression and coercion. These are fundamental differences. They reflect different beliefs about whether human beings can be said to own themselves, how they acquire property rights in natural resources, and what their well-being consists in.

Liberal legalists are at one chiefly in their common illusion that their views on rights do not express rival views of the good. In reality, Rawls and Hayek have opposed conceptions of justice, not because they take different stances in the philosophy of right, but because they hold to antagonistic conceptions of the good life. In their accounts, as in all theories of rights and justice, differing views of rights spring from different views of the good.

What these egalitarian and libertarian variants of liberal legalism have in common is more fundamental than the points at which they differ. Each supposes that principles of justice and rights can be formulated that are at once highly determinate and ideally universal. (That the later Rawls appears to have retreated from the ideal of universality does not affect the present argument.[7])

Libertarian liberals such as Nozick believe that a universal economic system is required by justice. For them, rights of property and laws of contract are not social and legal conventions, which can reasonably vary in accord with the changing requirements of human well-being. They are direct applications of universal human rights. It is not merely that modern economies cannot prosper without well-functioning market institutions. Rather, the institutions of the market embody timeless dictates of justice. Indeed, on this strange view, only a single type of market economy – the highly singular type of capitalism found intermittently in some English-speaking countries over the past century or so – is fully compatible with the demands of justice.[8]

Thinking of market freedoms in this way, as derivations from fundamental human rights, is a fundamental error. Like other human freedoms, the freedoms embodied in market institutions are justified inasmuch as they meet human needs. Insofar as they fail to do this they can reasonably be altered. This is true not only of the rights that are involved in market institutions. It is true of all human rights.

The institutions of the market advance human well-being

to the extent that they enable individuals and communities with different or incompatible goals and interests to trade with one another to mutual advantage. This classical defence of market institutions can be given another formulation. Individuals and communities animated by rival and (in part) incommensurable values can interact in markets without needing to reconcile these rival conceptions of the good. Market institutions assist personal autonomy and social pluralism by enabling such communities to replace destructive conflict by beneficial competition. In short, there is a value-pluralist defence of market institutions; but there is no one best variety of market institutions, either for every society, or for every context in a single society.

Markets are not free-standing. They are highly complex legal and cultural institutions. They do most to promote pluralism and autonomy when they are complemented by other, non-market institutions. Without the 'positive' freedoms conferred by enabling welfare institutions, the 'negative' liberties of the market are of limited value.[9]

Egalitarian liberals such as Rawls do not claim that only one kind of economic system can be just. They recognize that justice can be realized in a variety of economic systems. Depending on historical circumstances, sometimes socialism may be best, at others some species of capitalism. In Rawlsian theory, justice is silent on the choice of economic systems. Despite this, whatever system is chosen must satisfy Rawls's principles of distribution.[10]

This last requirement presupposes that an overlapping consensus on distributive issues can be reached across the numerous ways of life that exist in late modern societies. But insofar as different ways of life are animated by different ideals of the good, they will think of issues of distribution differently. A strongly individualist way of life will take for granted that the social unit of distribution is the individual. Others will nominate the family or intermediate social institutions for that purpose.

The several ways of life that may be found in most contemporary societies do not share a conception of the primary goods of human life. They are animated by different conceptions of the good life, which may overlap enough to make compromise possible, but which have too little in common to permit the development of a single, overarching conception of justice.

For liberal legalists, when different ways of life clash, all that needs to be done is to ask what justice demands. Once the principles governing an ideally liberal constitution have been stated, they need only to be applied. Applying the law is applying a theory of justice to particular cases; and there are no hard cases that cannot be decided. But when society contains not one but many ways of life, each with its own conception of the good, will there not be as much divergence in views of fairness as there is in understandings of the good? When ways of life differ widely in their view of the good, will they not support different views of justice?

Liberal legalists aim to circumvent conflict about the good life by appealing to ideas of justice and rights. In this they claim a lineage that goes back to Kant, who sought to develop a political philosophy based solely on the right. Whether or not this is a correct interpretation of Kant, a pure philosophy of right is a quixotic enterprise. The right can never be prior to the good. Without the content that can be given it only by a conception of the good, the right is empty.

A strictly political liberalism, which is dependent at no point on any view of the good, is an impossibility. The central catsegories of such a liberalism – 'rights', 'justice', and the like – have a content only insofar as they express a view of the good. At the same time, insofar as they have any definite content, claims about rights and justice are enmeshed in conflicts of value. If we differ about the good life, we are bound to differ about justice and rights. Political liberalism presupposes that justice can stand aloof from conflicting claims about the good. In truth the enterprise of a theory of justice is undone by these conflicts.

Recent liberal political philosophy ascribes infinite weight to a value that is almost infinitely complex. The requirements of justice are not everywhere the same. Because expectations vary from society to society, what is just in one may be unjust in another. What justice demands is not a matter of subjective preference, but it varies with history and circumstances.

Universal human values do not generate a single view of

justice. They frame constraints on what can count as a reasonable compromise between rival values and ways of life. In this way, universal human values set ethical limits on the pursuit of *modus vivendi*. Like liberal toleration, *modus vivendi* is far from being the idea that anything goes.

Peaceful coexistence is not an a priori value. In this it is no different from any other human good. It is desirable only insofar as it serves human goals and needs. There is no argument which shows that all ways of life are bound to pursue it. Nevertheless, nearly all ways of life have interests in common that make *modus vivendi* desirable for them. Even ways of life that do not recognize any ideal of toleration may have reason to seek peaceful coexistence. So, equally, do 'liberal' and 'non-liberal' regimes. Yet there are limits to *modus vivendi*.

Liberals and pluralists walk side by side in resisting totalitarian and fundamentalist regimes. *Modus vivendi* is impossible in a regime in which the varieties of the good are seen as symptoms of error or heresy. Without institutions in which different ways of life are accorded respect there cannot be peaceful coexistence between them. Where liberal regimes foster this coexistence, pluralists are bound to support them.

Nevertheless, when liberals set up one regime as a standard of legitimacy for all the rest, pluralists and liberals part company. For pluralists, a liberal regime may sometimes be the best framework for *modus vivendi*. At other times a non-liberal regime may do as well, or better.

The distinction between liberal and non-liberal regimes is not categorical; but that does not mean we cannot tell the difference between them. It means only that a liberal regime cannot be identified by reference to any set of common features. We distinguish liberal from illiberal regimes by a number of marks, none of which is possessed by all. We recognize liberal regimes not by their having any essential properties but by their family resemblances.

It is a mark of an illiberal regime that conflicts of value are viewed as signs of error. Yet liberal regimes which claim that one set of liberties – their own – is universally legitimate adopt precisely that view. They treat conflicts among liberties as symptoms of error, not dilemmas to which different solutions can be reasonable. Liberalism of this kind is a species of fundamentalism, not a remedy for it.

It is commonly held that value-pluralism supports liberalism as a political ideal. The truth is nearer the opposite. If a pluralist account of the human good is true, the claims of fundamentalist liberalism are spurious. From the standpoint of value-pluralism, all conflicts between rival claims about the best life for humankind are collisions of illusions. Universal religions fall into this category.[11] So do most Enlightenment political philosophies.

Inasmuch as they prescribe a single way of life, or a small family of ways of life, as being right or best for all humankind, universal religions are incompatible with the truth of value-pluralism. Common experience and the evidences of history show human beings thriving in forms of life that are very different from one another. None can reasonably claim to embody the flourishing that is uniquely human. If there is anything distinctive about the human species, it is that it can thrive in a variety of ways.

The truth that there are many varieties of human flourishing is no less incompatible with the universalist political projects that have emerged from the Enlightenment. Not only liberals, but Marxists and social democrats have held that the human good is such that it can only be fully embodied in a single, universal regime.[12] In their different ways, each of these political philosophies is committed to the Enlightenment project of a universal civilization.

To affirm that humans thrive in many different ways is not to deny that there are universal human values. Nor is it to reject the claim that there should be universal human rights. It is to deny that universal values can only be fully realized in a universal regime. Human rights can be respected in a variety of regimes, liberal and otherwise. Universal human rights are not an ideal constitution for a single regime throughout the world, but a set of minimum standards for peaceful coexistence among regimes that will always remain different.

Liberal universalists are right that some values are universal. They are wrong in identifying universal values with their own particular ideals. Human rights are not a charter giving universal authority to liberal values. They are a benchmark of minimal legitimacy for societies whose values are different.

Liberal relativists are wrong in thinking there are no universal values. They are right that liberal values belong in one way of life, or a family of ways of life, and have no universal authority. At the same time, they are mistaken in supposing that liberal societies can abandon their universalist claims without being altered profoundly.

Liberal societies claim to be the only legitimate embodiment of universal values. All others are judged as approximations to themselves. This claim to universal authority has entered deeply into the self-image of liberal cultures. Insofar as a pluralist view of human values spreads, it is bound to undermine this self-understanding.

Value-pluralism does not leave everything as it is. It is a subversive doctrine. It undermines all claims about the best life for the species. Accordingly, it is inimical to fundamentalism of every kind, whether it originates in religious faith or in the dogmas of the Enlightenment.

Totalitarian and fundamentalist regimes claim that conflicts of value are illusory – at any rate in the long run of history, or in heaven. If value-pluralism is true, that claim itself embodies an illusion. Pluralism about values undermines illiberal claims about harmony. At the same time, it works to subvert the self-interpretation of liberal cultures in which they are precursors of a universal regime or way of life.[13]

Universal values are not the ground of a universal civilization. Through their conflicts they explain the fact that no such thing has ever existed. The persistence of many ways of life is a natural response to species-wide conflicts. Humans are highly inventive animals. From universal conflicts they are continuously devising particular forms of life. Unless new technologies succeed in altering human endowments radically, this will always be true.

The belief that we are destined to live in a universal civilization is a commonplace in societies shaped by Enlightenment thinking. Yet it has scant support in history. In truth, it is not a result of historical inquiry, but rather the product of a discredited philosophy of history.

All political philosophies express a philosophy of history. This is most obviously true of those varieties of liberalism that deny possessing any such thing. The Rawlsian school affects a stance of neutrality or silence regarding questions in the philosophy of history. Yet Rawls's political philosophy can claim to be something more than the pursuit of the intimations of American academic liberals only if its account of the fact of pluralism fits a broad range of modern societies.

In truth, Rawls's interpretation of the fact of pluralism and his account of overlapping consensus are relevant to the majority of contemporary societies only if they are destined to become increasingly like the United States – as Rawls imagines it to be. In effect, this is to subscribe to a specific interpretation of history – an Americocentric version of a positivist philosophy which affirms that as societies become more modern they are bound to become more alike.

Describing the positivist interpretation of history, Stuart Hampshire writes: 'The positivists believed that all societies across the globe will gradually discard their traditional attachments . . . because of the need for rational, scientific and experimental modes of thought which a modern industrial economy involves. This is an old faith, widespread in the nineteenth century, that there must be a step-by-step convergence on liberal values, on "our values".' The difficulty with this theory, as Hampshire concludes, is that has been falsified by history: 'We now know there is no "must" about it and that all such theories have a predictive value of zero.'[14]

This positivist interpretation of history has had a practical influence. Since the last decades of the twentieth century many governments and some transnational institutions have formed their policies on the unexamined assumption that only one economic system is compatible with the requirements of modernity. In this, they are influenced by neoliberal ideologues who believe that in promoting the free market they are easing the birth of a universal economic system that history would anyway have made inevitable.

The idea that only one kind of economic system is compatible with modernity is of a piece with the notion that as different societies become more modern they are bound to become more alike. In fact, as different societies become more modern, they develop different modes of economic life. In Japan, modernization has meant not the replication of any other mode of economic life, but instead the development of an indigenous variety of capitalism which has many unique features. The same is true in India and China.

Subject to constraints of geography, competition and power, different societies develop modes of economic life that express their different ways of life. Where, as in most late modern societies, there are several ways of life, there tend to be a number of distinct types of productive enterprise, expressing different family structures, religious beliefs and values.

The notion that all modern economies are converging on a single mode of economic life does not square with history. It is a remnant of early nineteenth-century speculative sociology which became embedded in later thought. Like Marxists in the 1930s, contemporary neoliberals are unwitting disciples of a defunct positivist ideology.[15]

The belief that modern societies will everywhere converge on the same values does not result from historical inquiry. It is a confession of faith. In fact late modern societies show little evidence of any such consensus. They differ from each other too much.

There are many ways of being modern. Different societies absorb science and engender new technologies without accepting the same values. The idea that modern societies are much the same everywhere which is still defended by Enlightenment fundamentalists, has scant support in history. Like many of the hopes bequeathed by the Enlightenment, it is a fleeting shadow of monotheism.[16]

Liberal toleration is an ambiguous inheritance. From one side, it is an ideal of rational consensus. From the other, it is a solution to a problem of peaceful coexistence. These are not variations on a single ideal. They are rival projects, expressing rival philosophies – not least, rival philosophies of history.

In practical life, seeking compromise among irreconcilable aims is a mark of wisdom. In intellectual life, it is a sign of confusion. In present circumstances, attempting to preserve the liberal ideal of toleration as a means of reaching a rational consensus is harmful. It makes the practice of coexistence contingent on an expectation of increasing convergence in values that is fated to be disappointed.

If the liberal project is to be renewed, the ambiguity that has haunted it from its origins must be resolved. The idea of toleration as a means to a universal consensus on values must be given up, with the adoption instead of a project of *modus vivendi* among ways of life animated by permanently divergent values.

Like any other political philosophy, *modus vivendi* articulates a view of the good. It is an application of value-pluralism to political practice. It tells us to reject theories which promise a final resolution of moral conflicts, since their result in practice can only be to diminish the goods that have generated our conflicts.

When it is applied to the ethical life of individuals, value-pluralism suggests that seeking a compromise among values and ways of life whose claims cannot be fully reconciled need not be unreasonable. On the contrary, the struggle to honour incompatible claims may be a mark of the richness of our lives. Yet *modus vivendi* is a political project, not a moral ideal. It does not preach compromise as an ideal for all to follow. Nor does it aim to convert the world to value-pluralism. In these respects *modus vivendi* is far from any of the conventional varieties of liberalism.

The pursuit of *modus vivendi* is not a quest for some kind of super-value. It is a commitment to common institutions in which the claims of rival values can be reconciled. The end of *modus vivendi* is not any supreme good – even peace. It is reconciling conflicting goods. That is why *modus vivendi* can be pursued by ways of life having opposed views of the good.

The ideal of *modus vivendi* is not based on the vain hope that human beings will cease to make universal claims for their ways of life. It regards such claims with indifference – except where they endanger peaceful coexistence. In this, *modus vivendi* harks back to Thomas Hobbes. A Hobbesian state extends to private belief the radical tolerance of indifference. Hobbes is thereby the progenitor of a tradition of liberal thought in which *modus vivendi* is central.

The idea that Hobbes is one of the authors of liberalism may be unfamiliar to political philosophers whose education has not included a study of the history of the subject. But liberal thought did not begin a generation ago. Only ignorance of the longer history of liberal thought supports the belief in a single, continuous liberal tradition.

The proposition that principles of justice must be neutral regarding rival views of the good is treated as an axiom in the liberal orthodoxy of the past generation; but neither the term nor – more significantly – the idea of neutrality is to be found in liberal writings before the 1970s. In this, as in other ways, recent liberal thinking is discontinuous with what went before. Such shifts are not new in liberal thought. They occur throughout its history.

Just as liberal regimes cannot be identified by a range of essential properties, so liberal theories and thinkers are not alike in having common ideas. It is a basic error to search for the essence of something as heterogeneous and discontinuous as *the* liberal tradition. Liberalism is not the kind of thing that has an essence.[17]

The dangers of seeking to define an essential liberal tradition are well illustrated by Hayek's attempt to identify 'true' or 'classical' liberalism as a whiggish, 'English' tradition running from Locke to Adam Smith, which was swamped by a 'new' or 'French' liberalism towards the end of the eighteenth century.[18] Identifying David Hume and Adam Smith as English thinkers is only one of the oddities in this account. The Scottish Enlightenment to which Hume and Smith belonged was not a separate development, wholly detached from the French Enlightenment. Many of the formative influences in Hume's thought were French. Much in Hume's thought is a response to the sceptical tradition of early modern Pyrrhonism to which Michel de Montaigne belonged.[19] It is a mistake to represent Hume's philosophy as part of an indigenous 'English' intellectual tradition. Rather, it is a development in European thought. If there is a formative English influence on Hume, it is Hobbes – whom Hayek consigns to the 'French' tradition of Cartesian rationalism.[20] Again, Hayek's attempt to define a tradition of 'true' or 'classical' liberalism deforms the thought of Adam Smith. True, if anyone was a liberal in the late eighteenth century, it was Adam Smith; but he was just as much a critic of liberalism. Smith was an early critic of the moral hazards of commercial societies. Many of the criticisms of capitalism that were later developed by Marx – notably those concerning its alienating and stupefying effects on workers – are prefigured in Smith's thought. In fact, so far is Smith from being an exemplar of 'true' or 'classical' liberal thought that one could just as well say of him that he is one of the chief sources of later critiques of liberalism.[21]

Contrary to Hayek, no useful purpose is served by seeking to separate out 'false' from 'true' liberalism. Even so, we can clearly identify some thinkers as liberals and others as critics of liberalism. (And some – such as Adam Smith and Michael Oakeshott – as both.) If it is clear that Constant and de Tocqueville were liberals, it is equally evident that Rousseau and de Maistre were not. If Kant is a paradigm of a certain type of liberal thinker, Nietzsche is no less exemplary as a critic of liberalism. When James Fitzjames Stephen attacked John Stuart Mill, his target was the leading liberal thinker of the age.[22]

As we do with liberal and non-liberal regimes, we recognize these thinkers as belonging to a tradition of liberal thought not in virtue of their exhibiting a set of defining features but by their family resemblances. As we move back from the eighteenth to the seventeenth century, recognizing any liberal tradition becomes trickier. Yet even then some thinkers were unmistakably liberal and others manifestly not.

Locke belongs in a tradition of liberal argument on the limits of political authority, whereas Filmer is an opponent of that emerging tradition. For Filmer, political authority comes by right, ultimately divine, unlimited by the consent of the subject. For Locke it depends on consent – however obscurely consent is qualified by his vestigial medieval notions about natural law. In seeking to ground the authority of government on hypothetical individual choice, Locke looks forward to later thinkers who are without question liberals.

So does Hobbes – in some ways more unequivocally. By making the authority of government contingent on its success in protecting the vital interests of its subjects, Hobbes belongs more clearly with later liberal thought than does Locke. In truth, if one of the core projects of liberalism is a form of peaceful coexistence that is not held together by common beliefs, Hobbes is a liberal thinker *au fond*. Hobbes understood better than most of the liberal thinkers who followed him what the problem of coexistence was, and how far it could be solved. As Michael Oakeshott put it, 'without being himself a liberal, Hobbes had in him more of the philosophy of liberalism than many of its professed defenders.'[23]

So, too, did David Hume. In contrast to Locke, Hume did not seek to found society on shared beliefs. For Hume, society stands not on any foundation of first principles or common belief but on shared practices. As I have noted, Hume was much indebted to French Pyrrhonism. His resolution of the sceptical paradoxes propounded by the Pyrrhonists was itself sceptical: it accepted that nature and convention, not reason, sustain morality and society. Radical scepticism of this kind can easily lead to quietism (as it did in Montaigne). In Hume, however, it produced a species of liberal philosophy in which the conviction that society needs shared beliefs has been largely abandoned.[24]

The two rival liberal philosophies help us understand what is new in our present circumstances. Throughout much of their history they had a crucial assumption in common. Both affirmed that human nature was constant and invariant. Both assumed that the good life was the same for all humankind. After Mill, this became increasingly difficult to take for granted. A new element of cultural difference entered the old ambiguities of liberal toleration.

For Hobbes, 'commodious living' means much the same wherever it can be achieved. For Hume, 'civilization' has always been animated by the same values. For both, politics was the pursuit of a peaceful accommodation of competing human interests; and, for both, the interests of human beings are everywhere much the same. In this last belief, Hobbes and Hume were at one with Locke and Kant, the chief exemplars of the rival liberal philosophy of rational consensus. None of these thinkers doubted that the good life was something singular, univocal and universal – even when they recognized, as Kant surely did, that its ingredients were often in conflict.

The faith that the good life is the same for all humankind is far from being universal or immemorial. In Europe, however, it prevailed until the time of the Romantics, when – led by such thinkers as Herder – it began to be questioned, then abandoned. As this faith gave way, the idea of 'civilization' was supplanted by that of 'culture'.[25]

The idea of 'culture' suggests that the forms of life in which humans can flourish are inherently various. It enters liberalism from German post-Romantic thought, notably that of Wilhelm von Humboldt. It becomes a central liberal theme only with John Stuart Mill.[26]

Mill's thought contains something of each of the rival liberal philosophies. At times, he is a militant partisan of an Enlightenment faith according to which the best way of life is the same for all – the form of life of autonomous individuals. At other times, Mill is a hesitant critic of this liberal Enlightenment faith. Influenced by Humboldt's arguments for 'the absolute and essential importance of human development in its richest diversity', which he quoted as the epigraph to *On Liberty*, Mill wrote: ' "Pagan self-assertion" is one of the elements of human worth, as well as "Christian self-denial". There is a Greek ideal of self-development, which the Platonic and Christian ideal of self-government blends with, but does not supersede.'[27] In such statements, Mill is not far from accepting that human beings can flourish in divergent forms of life whose worth cannot be compared.

Mill spent much of his life trying to reconcile his Enlightenment project of a universal civilization with his post-Romantic suspicion that it endangered freedom and diversity.[28] His suspicion was that if liberal toleration is based on the pursuit of such a consensus might it itself become illiberal. If diversity in ways of life has merely heuristic value as a means of discovering the best life, it is endangered by intellectual progress. A liberal society has no value in itself. It is no more than a stage on the way to a rational consensus. In that case, as humankind progresses, liberal values are bound to become obsolete. This was a result the French positivists were happy to accept when they argued that freedom is no more necessary in morality than it is in chemistry.[29]

On Liberty was Mill's attempt to develop an argument for freedom that does not have this self-undermining effect. He was only partly successful. Mill's *Essay* is haunted by the ambiguity that runs throughout the liberal tradition. Insofar as Mill held to the faith that one form of life is best for humankind, he sought to defend toleration of different ways of living as a path to truth. In this Mill held to a version of the Enlightenment project in which liberal institutions are defended not so much as embodiments of a particular conception of it as means of inquiry into it. At the same time he sought to avoid the self-undermining effect of justifying liberal institutions as a means to truth by claiming that humans can thrive in different and incompatible forms of life. In this view, which Mill imbibed from the German Romantics, rival values need not stand to one another in a relation of truth and falsity. They may point to different ways in which humans can live well. In favouring liberal institutions as instruments of inquiry, Mill looked forward to a rational consensus on the best way for humans to live. In affirming that humans can live well in a variety of ways he was a proto-value-pluralist. Mill's project in *On Liberty* founders between these two philosophies.

Assessing Mill's argument in *On Liberty*, Isaiah Berlin wrote:

> His argument is plausible only on the assumption which, whether he knew it or not, Mill all too obviously made, that human knowledge was in principle never complete, and always fallible; that there was no single, universally visible truth; that each man, each nation, each civilisation, might take its own road towards its own goal, not necessarily harmonious with those of others; that men are altered, and the truths in which they believe are altered, by new experiences and their own actions – what he calls 'experiments in living': that consequently the conviction, common to Aristotelians and atheistical materialists alike, that there exists a basic knowable human nature, one and the same, at all times, in all places, in all men – a static, unchanging substance underneath all the altering

appearances, with permanent needs, dictated by a single, discoverable goal, or pattern of goals, the same for all mankind – is mistaken.[30]

By tacitly abandoning the assumptions that underpin the liberalism of rational consensus, Mill came close to affirming a philosophy of liberal pluralism, or *modus vivendi*. Yet in so doing he did not look back to Hobbes or Hume. He looked forward to a time when the common assumption not only of Hobbes and Hume but also of Locke and Kant – that humans flourish best in a single, universal civilization – could no longer be sustained. By affirming that the human good is found in divergent forms of life, Mill opened the way for a variety of liberal thought in which the idea of a universal civilization has no place.

In 'Two Concepts of Liberty' Berlin took up where Mill left off. Berlin sought to ground the value of liberty in the same plurality of ideals and forms of life that defeated Mill's enterprise in *On Liberty*. He defended liberty not because it enables the discovery of the one true way for humans to flourish, but because it allows people to flourish in different ways.

Nor was this merely a diversity of personal lifestyles. Berlin recognized that, for nearly all human beings, living well involved participation in particular ways of life. For Berlin, human flourishing required peaceful coexistence among different cultures, not their merging into a universal civilization. He never imagined that a world of distinctive ways of life could exist without deep and sometimes tragic conflicts.

There are many difficulties in the account of liberal thought that is implicit in Berlin's writings. At some points in 'Two Concepts of Liberty', he seems to suggest that a commitment to negative liberty in terms of non-interference embodies true liberal values, with positive conceptions of liberty as personal autonomy representing a departure from this position. Against this, some thinkers who are liberals by any standard, such as John Stuart Mill, hold to a more positive view of liberty, while others who stand outside of liberal thought, however laxly construed, such as Jeremy Bentham, adopt a negative view. It is legitimate to seek to understand liberal thought in terms of the ideas of freedom that are found in it, but none of them is the key that unlocks liberalism's 'true' values.

On the other hand, Berlin's recognition that conflicts of value break out within liberty itself marks a new development in liberal thought. Unlike most liberal thinkers, Berlin understood that liberty is not one thing but many, that its various components do not all mesh together but often clash, that when they do conflict there is inevitably loss and sometimes no solution that all reasonable people are bound to accept. The result is a profoundly instructive philosophy of agonistic liberalism.[31]

Yet, as I will show, Berlin's attempt to ground liberalism in a value-pluralist ethical theory breaks down in much the same way as did Mill's attempt to construct a liberal utilitarianism. If there are irreducibly many values which cannot be ranked or weighed on any single scale, negative liberty – which Berlin sees as the core liberal value – can be only one good among many. If, furthermore, there are incommensurable sorts of negative liberty, then different regimes can rightly protect different mixes of liberties. Yet again, if there are incommensurable kinds of liberty, there cannot be on-balance, comparative judgements about 'the greatest liberty'. In that case, it cannot be true that the best regime is that which promotes the greatest liberty. For if there are many incommensurable liberties, maximal liberty has no meaning.

The impossibility of deriving the priority of negative liberty over other values from value-pluralism can be seen as a defeat for liberalism. That was how Michael Oakeshott understood the failure of John Stuart Mill's enterprise of deriving a principle of liberty from utilitarianism. Oakeshott claimed that, because Mill could not defend the 'one very simple principle' he sought in *On Liberty*, he 'abandoned reference to general principles as a reliable guide in political activity'.[32]

Oakeshott understood this as a defeat for liberalism. In fact, Oakeshott's political philosophy was itself closer to liberalism than to any other – but it was a version of the liberalism of *modus vivendi*.[33] His mistake was to suppose that liberalism must be understood as a system of principles, and to seek to replace reference to principle by the guidance of tradition – as if any late modern society, least of all his own, contained only one tradition. If contemporary societies contain several traditions, with many people belonging to more than one, politics cannot be conducted by following any one tradition. It must try to reconcile the intimations of rival traditions. As Hobbes understood, it must seek *modus vivendi*.[34]

We need not see the failure of Mill's enterprise, or of Berlin's, as the failure of liberalism. Instead of seeing liberalism as a system of universal principles, we can think of it as the enterprise of pursuing terms of coexistence among different ways of life. Instead of thinking of liberal values as if they were universally authoritative, we can think of liberalism as the project of reconciling the claims of conflicting values. If we do this, liberal philosophy will look not to an illusion of universal consensus, but instead to the possibilities of *modus vivendi*. If we think of liberalism in these terms, we will take a further step in an intellectual pilgrimage begun by John Stuart Mill and continued in our own time by Isaiah Berlin, and resolve an ambivalence that has beset liberalism throughout its history.

Because *modus vivendi* rejects the claim of liberal values to universal authority, it is bound to be at odds with the prevailing philosophy of liberal toleration. Yet *modus vivendi* can still claim to be a renewal of the liberal project. For it continues the search for peace that liberal toleration began.

2

Plural Values

The human good is shown in rival ways of living. This is no longer only a claim in moral philosophy. It is a fact of ethical life. Today we know that human beings flourish in conflicting ways, not from the detached standpoint of an ideal observer, but as a matter of common experience. As migration and communication have commingled ways of life that used to be distinct and separate, the contention of values has become our common condition. For us, pluralism is an historical fate.

Yet value-pluralism was a truth about human life before it was an inescapable social condition. There have been many attempts to explicate it.[1] What all have in common is the proposition that there are many kinds of good life, some of which cannot be compared in worth. Some varieties of the good life are neither better nor worse than each other, nor the same in value, but incommensurable; they are differently valuable. Similarly, some regimes are neither more nor less legitimate than one another. They are legitimate for different reasons.

From Locke and Kant to Rawls and Hayek, a line of liberal thinkers have accepted that the goods of life clash, with no settlement of their claims being without loss; but they have sought to state principles of right and justice that stand aloof from these conflicts. If, however, the claims of justice embody values that are themselves incompatible and incommensurable, that version of the liberal project runs aground. We should adopt a liberal philosophy whose guiding ideal is not the chimera of rational consensus, or an idea of reasonable disagreement, but *modus vivendi* among ways of life that will always be different.

Much of this chapter will be spent trying to clarify the elusive idea of incommensurability. Here I note only that value-pluralism is a view that aims for fidelity to ethical life. If ethical life contains conflicts of value that are rationally undecidable, that is a truth we must accept – not something we should seek to tidy away for the sake of theoretical consistency.

Value-pluralism is an account of ethical life as we find it. At the same time value-pluralism does not claim that ethical life has to be the way it is. Human nature could have been other than we know it to be, and it is not impossible that it should cease to be as it is. In ethics there are no a priori truths. In that sense, ethics cannot be other than an empirical inquiry.

Incommensurable values arise in a variety of ways, of which three are relevant to the present inquiry. First, incommensurable goods arise from the conventions that govern moral life in particular cultures. It is part of the meaning of some goods that they are not to be traded off against one another. Such goods are constituted by conventions which forbid their being exchanged for one another. Second, incommensurable values can arise when the same good is differently interpreted in different cultures. In art, we can identify the best among works belonging to the same genre, yet their styles may be too far apart for any judgement of relative worth among the best to be a possibility. Much the same holds in ethics. Third, incommensurable values arise when different goods and virtues are honoured in different cultures. Cultures differ not only in how they interpret virtues they have in common but in the virtues they recognize. What some praise as virtuous others may condemn as a vice. When cultures honour different virtues, it is sometimes impossible to compare the value of the ways of life in which they are embodied.

However they arise, goods that are incommensurable cannot be compared in overall value. Consider friendship. Insofar as someone charges money for the time he spends with others, he is not a friend. It is part of friendship not to exchange the time one spends with friends for money. This does not mean that friendship must be ranked over any amount of money. To say that friendship and money are incomparable in value does not mean that having friends is incomparably better than having money. It means that friendship and money cannot be compared in value. As Joseph Raz has put it: 'Only those who hold the view that friendship is neither better nor worse than money, but is simply not comparable to money or other commodities are *capable* of having friends. Similarly only those who would not even consider exchanges of money for friendship are capable of having friends.'[2]

To have to buy friendship is a pitiable condition. It is pitiable not because friendship is worth infinitely more than money, but because friends – unlike psychotherapists and sexual partners, say – cannot be bought. To be sure, one who understands that friends cannot be bought may, if compelled to choose between friendship and goods that can be bought, choose the latter in some contexts of her life. If she does so, she is not exchanging something that has infinite value for something that has a lesser value. She is choosing a life in which friendship has a lesser place than other goods. She may have good reason to do so.

The life of someone who has chosen goods that can be bought over goods that cannot be bought need not be poorer than that of someone who has made the contrary choice. If goods such as friendship and money cannot be compared in value, neither can the lives of people who make different choices between them. Yet such choices are not arbitrary. Our histories and circumstances, our needs and goals, may give good reasons for different choices.

The value that friendship and money have for any of us is agent-relative; but that does not make it entirely subjective. I may be right to prefer friendship over money and you may be mistaken to do so – and vice versa. The best lives may be – as Aristotle thought – mixed lives containing many goods. Contrary to what Aristotle may have believed, however, there need be no best combination of goods, even in a single life.[3]

The incommensurability of friendship and money is a convention in many societies. To be sure, there are significant variations in the stringency with which it is applied. Friendships in which pecuniary gain is a central ingredient have been acknowledged by many cultures, including the Greeks and Romans. Aristotle acknowledged friendships which depend on mutual benefit of this kind, though he regarded them as less valuable than friendships in which each values the other for his own sake. Epicurus' ideal of friendship was highly instrumental.

We can see that Aristotle and Epicurus are speaking of the same good – one that we prize; but at the same time it is sufficiently different for comparative judgements of the worth of ancient and modern friendship to be impossible. Here we have an example of a second way in which incommensurable values can arise – when the same good is differently construed and embodied in different cultures.

Consider some examples from the arts. Aeschylus, Shakespeare and Samuel Beckett are supremely great dramatists; but we cannot rank their work in value. The cultural contexts of their plays are too different. Similarly, we can recognize the Temple of Poseidon at Sounion and the Zen garden at Ryonanji to be supreme examples of religious architecture; but we cannot compare their worth, because their backgrounds and styles are too far removed from one another.

There is a parallel with the virtues. Without some virtues no human life can thrive. Such virtues as courage and prudence are generically human. Yet they are differently embodied in different cultures.

Courage among the Zulu is something different from courage among the Quakers; but it is courage all the same. As between the Zulu warrior who goes into battle against high or impossible odds and the Quaker stretcher-carrier who risks his life in the trenches, no judgement of comparative bravery can be made. One is not better than the other, nor are the two roughly the same in value. In the same way, we cannot rank the research scientist who takes part in a dangerous medical experiment against the social reformer who takes up a truly unpopular cause. We can say only that they are different exemplars of a universal virtue. (That does not mean it is always easy to distinguish between different interpretations of a universal human virtue and the different virtues of particular cultures.)

The third way in which incommensurable values arise is found when different goods and virtues are realized in different ways of life. The ideals of life we find honoured across longer stretches of history and in disparate cultures are irreducibly diverse; some of them are necessarily discordant; and reasonable people do not converge on any ranking of them.

Think of the virtues that animate the *Iliad* and those that inform the Sermon on the Mount. Heroic excellence in Homer (*arete*) and the New Testament virtue of loving-kindness (*agape*) are rivals. Bruno Snell has characterized the archaic Greek notion of *arete* thus:

> *Aretan* is 'to thrive'; *arete* is the objective which the early nobles attach to achievement and success. By means of *arete* the aristocrat implements the ideal of his order – and at the same time distinguishes himself above his fellow nobles. With his *arete* the individual subjects himself to the judgement of his community, but he also surpasses it as an individual.[4]

It is difficult to think of an ideal more at odds with the virtues of the Sermon on the Mount. *Agape* requires virtue without return, save in the eyes of God. *Arete* is an agonistic virtue, in that those who possess it must outdo others in the eyes of the world. The lives of people exhibiting these virtues are mutually exclusive, since each requires what the other condemns. Much the same can be said of the virtues of the Old and the New Testament.

Equally, the warrior virtues that are celebrated in the *Iliad* and the self-examination practised by Socratic inquirers; the virtues of duty and detachment exemplified in the *Bhagavad-Gita* and the universal compassion preached by the Buddha; the ideal of self-creation which is articulated in Proust's *Remembrance of Things Past* and the holy simplicity embodied in Alyosha in Dostoevsky's *Brothers Karamazov* – these ideals are rivals. This is not only because they involve the cultivation of attitudes and dispositions that do not coexist easily in the same person. It is because the virtues of some are the vices of others.

The ideals of life that we find honoured in different cultures cannot be fused into one all-encompassing human good. Partly this is because, human nature being what it is, some virtues crowd out others. It is hard, if not altogether impossible, for a profoundly compassionate person to be at the same time dispassionately just. The psychological responses of empathy and detachment that go with these virtues drive one another out. Whatever may have been claimed from Aristotle up to the present, the unity of the virtues is a fiction.

There is a scarcity in the soul such that no human life can display all of the virtues. Yet it is not because of any narrowness in human nature that the many ideals of life cannot be merged into one. It is by necessity. What some ideals praise, others disparage. Some virtues and some vices are generically human; but what some cultures honour as virtuous others condemn as vicious. Different ways of life not only interpret universal virtues in different ways; they honour opposed virtues. Some of these virtues cannot be other than rivals. Yet each has been pursued by reasonable people.

The best life for human beings comes in many varieties, some of which cannot be combined. There is no one best or maximal form of life for humans. As Raz has written,

> A form of life is maximal if, under normal circumstances, a person whose life is of that kind cannot improve it by acquiring additional virtues, nor by enhancing the degree to which he possesses any virtue without sacrificing another virtue he possesses or the degree to which it is present in his life. Belief in value-pluralism is the belief that there are several maximal forms of life.[5]

If rational inquiry has failed to produce agreement on the best life, it is not because of any imperfection in human reason. It is because the idea of perfection has no sense in human life. As Isaiah Berlin put it, 'To admit that the fulfilment of some of our ideals may in principle make the fulfilment of others impossible is to say that the notion of total human fulfilment is a formal contradiction, a metaphysical chimera. . . . That we cannot have everything is a necessary, not a contingent, truth.'[6]

This third kind of incommensurability arises when different cultures honour different goods and virtues. Different cultural ideals of marriage are a familiar example. In many traditional societies, most marriages are arranged, and the ideal of romantic love is absent, or rejected, at least in its applications to marriage and family life. The basis of marriage is sought in personal and social compatibility, and the economic benefits reaped by the partners and their families are accepted as relevant considerations when judging the desirability of a match. By contrast, liberal cultures reject ideals of marriage in which personal choice and romantic love are not central. (At any rate, that is how they profess to see themselves.) What we have here is not a cultural variation on a shared ideal. Rather, there are different and opposed ideals.

It is not always easy to distinguish these three sources of incommensurability. When ways of life are commingled, incommensurable values are a common experience. In this respect the pluralism of late modern societies is different from that discussed by the thinkers by whom value-pluralism was first clearly stated.

Vico, Herder and Montesquieu attributed incommensurable values to cultures, traditions or ways of life isolated from one another by time or distance. Vico argued that a supreme effort of imagination was needed to grasp the moral ideas of the Homeric world, Montesquieu contrasted the ethical life of the Persians (as he imagined it to be) with that of the France he knew, while Herder wrote of unique cultures that could not be fused together in a universal civilization. For these writers, the incommensurability of values was an anthropological or historical truth, to be apprehended from the detached viewpoint of an impartial spectator. Among us, it is common knowledge.

It may be worth saying something about what incommensurable values are *not*. Incommensurability is *not* vagueness. All 'values' – conceptions of the good, duties, rights, ideals, virtues, whatever – are surrounded by some vagueness. In this they are no different from 'facts'. Indeterminacy is a feature of language, not a special property of value-judgements. To say that values are incommensurate is *not* to say that they are indeterminate. On the contrary, we can say that they are incommensurate only when we know that all relevant indeterminacies have been filtered out. When we say of peace and justice that their demands are incommensurable we do not mean we are in any doubt about what they demand. We mean we are in no doubt about what they demand – and that, when their demands conflict, there is no settlement of the conflict that is uniquely right or best.

Again, to say that there are incommensurable values does *not* mean that the only way we can test our ethical beliefs is by assessing their consistency with one another. Indeed it is to say virtually the opposite. Contrary to the fashionable notion that we should aim at a reflective equilibrium between our overall conception of the good and our particular moral responses, consistency is not an overriding virtue in ethics. As I shall show, our ethical beliefs may be in error in that they may be overturned by experience. The test of our ethical beliefs is not their consistency with one another, or with any theory, but their fidelity to ethical life.

Yet again, to claim that some values are incommensurable does *not* mean all values are equally valid. Incommensurability is a relational property. Two goods that are incommensurable as a pair may be commensurate when either or both are compared with other goods. Affirming that some particular ways of life cannot be compared in value with one another in no way implies that all ways of life are equally valuable. At the same time, to claim that goods are incommensurable is *not* to rank them. It is to say they cannot be ranked. Nor is it to accord them some kind of unique weight. It is to say that in relation to each other they cannot be given a weight.

To say of goods that their value is incommensurable does not mean that one is incomparably more valuable than the other. It means that no such comparison is possible. Nor does the claim that two goods have incommensurable value mean that such goods cannot be compared *tout court*. They can be compared endlessly – but they cannot be compared with one another in overall value.

To be sure, every good can be compared in value with some other good. We can always give goods some kind of ranking; often we can also attach weights to the goods we have thereby ranked. When we say of goods that their value cannot be compared, we mean that their value cannot be compared *with each other* – not, absurdly, that their value cannot be compared with that of any other good. To say that two goods cannot be compared in value does not mean that there are no contexts in which their value can be compared. It means that their value can only be compared in particular contexts.

That the value of goods cannot be compared is no bar to reasoning about them. We can judge the life of a crack addict to be poorer than that of both a carer in a leprosarium and a skilful *bon viveur* without being able to rank the carer's against the hedonist's. This does not mean that the value of the carer's and the hedonist's lives are roughly equal. It means that, though they can be ranked as a pair against the life of the crack addict, they cannot be ranked in value against each other. Let us add another life to the argument – Gauguin's. If it is true that the worth of the life of a carer cannot be compared with that of a *bon viveur*, nor that of a *bon viveur* with Gauguin's, then the carer's and Gauguin's life will also be incommensurable.

We can have good reasons for choosing between incommensurable goods that are at odds. Think of friendship and justice. These are incommensurable goods whose claims may be mutually exclusive. I do not mean here that questions of justice cannot arise in a friendship. I mean that what friendship demands may be incompatible with justice. To affirm that justice and friendship are incommensurable goods is not to claim that justice always ranks higher than friendship – or the contrary. It is to claim that they cannot be ranked. But that does not mean that if we have to choose between them we must do so without reason.

Say I have an understanding with a close friend to be on hand when she is in serious trouble; but that in the circumstances this is an understanding I can honour only by defaulting on a contractual engagement I have made to a business enterprise. What should I do? There is no answer that is right for every person or every circumstance; but what I do may still be right or wrong.

I may try to assess the impact on the interests of my friend and the business of failing to honour each engagement. Further, I may consider how defaulting on each of them meshes with my goals. How significant a role do I expect my friend and my business relationships to play in the life I aim to lead? These considerations may tell in favour of one course of action. My decision in cases such as this need not be arbitrary or groundless, an *acte gratuite* for which no reason can be given. Nor need it be the expression of a sheer preference. Given the context of my history and circumstances, my choice may be right or wrong.

Outside of their contexts in social practices, no value can be attached to goods such as justice and friendship. They acquire their meaning and worth from the histories, needs and goals of human subjects and the ways of life to which they belong. Conflicts of value arise only in contexts given by forms of common life. As Wittgenstein put it, 'If language is to be a means of communication, there must be agreement not only in definitions but also (queer as it sounds) in judgements.'[7] We can be at odds only if we have something in common.

Yet the context in which we resolve conflicts among incommensurable values cannot be taken as given. We can resolve conflicts among such goods by breaking down the conventions that engender them. As I suggest later in this chapter, such cases are the empirical kernel of the Nietzschean idea of radical choice.

When social conventions cease to serve the well-being of those subject to them, it may be time to revise them. Rebels and social reformers often do this, sometimes with good reason. If a code of honour makes demands whose effect is to threaten the well-being of loved ones, there may be reason to dissolve the code of honour which generates that conflict.

Not all incommensurable goods promote the well-being of people entrained by the practices that generate them. By altering social conventions, we can dissipate conflicts among incomparable goods. Sometimes little of importance is thereby lost; but we can easily imagine a society in which human life has been impoverished by the dissolution of social conventions in which the exchange of some goods is prohibited.

A society that contained neither justice nor friendship would be free of the tragic conflicts that arise between them; but this would be the freedom from tragedy that goes with utter poverty, not that which comes from having an abundance of options. A world in which everything can be traded is by necessity a world in which some goods cannot be had.

Like friendship, justice is constituted by a set of social conventions. Among these are prohibitions blocking the sale of trial verdicts for money. Countries in which justice is for sale are countries in which there is no justice. A world in which all goods were for sale would not be one in which goods which had once been impossible to exchange for money could now be bought and sold. It would be a world in which many goods had ceased to exist.

Social reformers and revolutionaries often try to restore incomparable goods that have existed in the past – and establish them where they have not existed before. When they proscribed slavery, abolitionists made persons and chattels incomparably valuable. As a result, human beings can neither be bought nor sold – even when the exchange is one to which they consent.

Incommensurable goods are by no means always constituted by social conventions. Some are anthropological universals. But universal human values are often rivals. When universal values collide there are no universal principles for settling their conflicts. (I leave aside, but not because it is unimportant, whether incommensurable goods and bads are found in the lives of other animals.)

To be at risk of violent death at the hands of other human beings is a great impediment to any kind of flourishing; but it cannot be, as Hobbes believed, the supreme evil of human life. Life-long undernourishment can be no less of an obstacle to well-being (and to long life). Which is better – a regime which ensures peace but in which many are malnourished or one that is plagued by fatal violence but in which no-one

starves? There is no answer that all reasonable people are bound
to accept.

Many ethical theories aim to make all goods commensurable. Utilitarianism is perhaps the most familiar example. A
utilitarian can allow that the value of some goods cannot be
compared; but he cannot admit that to be a common occurrence. If he did, utilitarianism would itself be useless.
Benthamite utilitarianism and more recent, indirect utilitarian theories aim to develop a calculus enabling all goods to be
traded off against one another and the result of the trade-off
assigned an overall value.

A value-pluralist need not deny that such a utilitarian calculus can be constructed. Goods that are irreducibly distinct
can always be made interchangeable by being represented as
tokens of a single type of value. It is not impossibly difficult to
render the goods that make up happy human lives into a utilitarian notation. The price of doing so, though, is to drain
significance from some of the deepest conflicts that ethical
life contains.

A utilitarian would represent the conflict between friendship and justice which I discussed earlier in the jargon of preferences and their satisfaction. The best resolution of such
conflicts, he would contend, is that which maximizes the satisfaction of preferences. The objection to this utilitarian calculus is like that against a society in which all goods can be
traded. Utilitarian theories that represent conflicts of value in
terms of the satisfaction of our preferences may render ethical life more coherent, but they do so at the price of impoverishing it.

A utilitarian calculus in which all values are interchangeable is bound to pass over the most important facts about our
preferences, which have to do with the reasons we hold to
them. Our preferences regarding our friends and the demands
of justice are not brute wants; they express our beliefs about
how our lives are to be lived. Utilitarian assessments can fac-
tor in the intensity of our preferences, but they are bound to
disregard the ways in which they express our beliefs about
how our lives should go. They cannot avoid assimilating preferences that express our ethical beliefs to wants – for a cold

drink on a hot day, say – for which no reason needs to be given.

Editing out our reasons for our preferences from our assessments of them surely makes ethical life more amenable to utilitarian calculation; but it does so by deforming it. In this, utilitarianism resembles subjectivist theories of morality which seek to resolve conflicts among incommensurable values by making personal preferences the final considerations in practical reasoning.

Theories of rights seek to suppress the reality of conflicts of value in a different way. Kantian theorists deny that the right action can ever contain wrong. For them, morality consists in a set of compossible injunctions. 'Ought implies can', they tell us, so it cannot be true that we ought to perform actions which are jointly impossible. Kantians accept that not all good things can be realized; some will crowd out others. Kant himself acknowledged that the great goods of life cannot live together. But, like his followers today, he insisted that doing right can never mean committing wrong.

Often, this view is associated with the claim that the requirements of the most central parts of morality – supposedly those having to do with the demands of justice – are infinitely weightier than those which have to do with what is merely desirable. In this Kantian account, the demands of justice are incomparably weightier than those of the rest of morality, with which they may conflict; but justice itself can never make conflicting demands.

The objection to all such accounts is that they displace the facts of ethical life for the sake of a mere theory. What is the authority of theory when it has this result? It is a matter of common experience that some practical and moral dilemmas cannot be resolved without irreparable loss. Why should consistency be pursued at the cost of fidelity to experience?

To be sure, just as rival goods can be made interchangeable in a utilitarian calculus, so theories of rights can always be made more consistent by removing from them rights that make incompatible claims; but the result is that rights no longer track the human interests they exist to protect. Nothing is easier than resolving a conflict among rights by deleting one of them. To do so, however, is to suppress the source of the conflict in ethical life – the fact that vital human interests are at odds. Since each and every right protects interests that may be at odds, the end of the road for this strategy is an account of rights that is so far removed from the facts of ethical life as to be practically vacuous.

When a British wartime minister sacked his entire typing pool on discovering that one of them (he did not know which) was leaking information to the enemy, he admitted that he was doing something horribly unfair. He declared that he was inflicting a lifelong injustice on all but one of the typists, but that he believed it to be the right action in the circumstances, despite the fact that it contained irreparable wrong.[8]

Despite their seemingly opposed views of moral reasoning, Kantian accounts of rights and utilitarian theories are at one in purporting to resolve dilemmas such as that of the British minister in ways that incur no loss. They achieve that objective only at the price of extinguishing the goods that generate such dilemmas. From the standpoint of Kantian and utilitarian theory, the minister was merely confused. Either he did the right thing and committed no wrong, or what he did was simply wrong. From a value-pluralist standpoint, by contrast, the minister was admirably responsive to the irreconcilable ethical demands of the situation. No theoretical construction – Kantian or utilitarian – matches his account in faithfulness to ethical life.

Kantianism and utilitarianism distort our view of ethical life in obedience to a misguided ideal of consistency. To be sure, in some of the sciences and in some contexts of practical life, consistency is a virtue. But why should we seek it in morality, if the result is to desolate ethical life? The answer may be that without consistency there can be nothing that resembles a theory. In that case, it is the enterprise of a theory of ethics that should be abandoned.

Liberal theories pretend to resolve conflicts among the goods that are honoured in liberal morality. All liberals acknowledge liberty and equality to be fundamental goods. Liberal theories of justice and rights attempt to show either that these goods cannot be rivals or that there are universally authoritative principles governing the resolution of their conflicts. The claim of liberal political philosophers to have formulated principles of right which avoid such conflicts cannot be sustained. Yet we can reason well or badly about conflicts of values in the absence of such 'principles' or any 'theory' of justice or rights.

Many philosophers reject the very idea of incommensurability. It would be strange were this not so. Incommensurability mocks the hopes that founded philosophy. If there are incommensurable values, the Socratic project of a rational reconstruction of ethical life must be abandoned, or at least amended. Yet incommensurable values do not subvert reason in ethics. They undermine an erroneous view of reason.

Resistance to incommensurability is supported by two common misunderstandings. One confuses incommensurability with the existence of entire moral outlooks, conceptual frameworks or *Weltanschauungen*. It imagines our moral judgements to be components of comprehensive views of the world, so different from one another that they are mutually unintelligible. This view interprets incommensurability as meaning that our moral outlooks are embodied in different world-views. Accordingly, we cannot reason about them. Rather, each of us is trapped in one of them. Let us call this view *relativism*.

Another, parallel interpretation sees talk of incommensurable values as a euphemism for the primacy of personal preferences. When incommensurable values conflict, it insists that is our wants that decide what is to be done. If reason cannot settle the issue, only our personal preferences can do so. Let us call this view *subjectivism*.

Both interpretations are mistaken. Relativists and subjectivists each deny that we can make reasonable choices among incommensurable values. What these interpretations have in common is the belief that there cannot be rational choices among incommensurable values. Both assume that a rational choice is one that adopts a single solution as being right. By contrast, what value-pluralism affirms is that in conflicts among incommensurable values incompatible choices can be right.

Our miscellaneous and disparate ideals and values cannot be ordered into a self-consistent theoretical system. Not only do we not possess such a system; the strongest claimants to be such a system break down on conflicts of value. It is not merely that such theories are not in themselves particularly compelling. Worse, they are disabled by the very conflicts of value they seek to deny. As I shall show in chapter 3, this is the fate of the most celebrated recent challenge to value-pluralism in political thought, John Rawls's theory of justice.

The demand for systematic rationality in ethical life comes from seeking to reconstruct practical reasoning in accordance with the requirements of theoretical consistency. Michael Oakeshott captured the inherently miscellaneous and incompletely consistent character of practical reasoning when he wrote:

> In reflecting upon a response to a practical situation . . . what we bring with us is a variety of beliefs – approvals and disapprovals, preferences and aversions, pro- and con- feelings (often vague), moral and prudential maxims of varying application and importance, hopes, fears, anxieties, skill in estimating the probable consequence of actions, and some general beliefs about the world. These beliefs, insofar as they are normative, are not self-consistent; they often pull in different directions, they compete with one another and cannot all be satisfied at the same time, and therefore they cannot properly be thought of as a norm or as a self-consistent set of norms or 'principles' capable of delivering to us an unequivocal message about what we should do. (We believe, for example, that the administration of justice should be speedy, careful, inexpensive, public, as little onerous as may be upon those absolved from offence, capable of reaching a definite conclusion, etc., etc.) Even to think of them as a creed gives them a character they have not got. Aristotle called them the 'admitted goods' and recognised them to be incommensurable. I call them a 'tradition', meaning to indicate that these beliefs were not a self-consistent set of 'principles', that although they might be expected to be relatively stable they were not incapable of change, that they were not axioms but maxims which we believed ourselves to have learnt from experience, and that they did not all appear before us in the form of propositions but often in institutions and practices.[9]

For those who believe that practical reasoning must satisfy the standards of consistency that supposedly apply in scientific theories, Oakeshott's acknowledgement of the place of incommensurables in practical reasoning is an admission that ethics can never be fully rational. Yet, as Oakeshott understood, it is not ethical life that is at fault. It is a mistaken ideal of rationality.

The argument that rationality and incommensurability are at odds has force only if our moral ideas are elements in comprehensive conceptual schemes. Now it is true that there can be, and are, profoundly different ideas of the virtues and of the good life; but they are not elements in well-ordered systems. Moral notions hang together loosely, like the forms of ethical life they express. We do not need a comprehensive scheme of 'moral concepts' in order to reason about ethical questions. On the contrary, we can reason about ethical questions only because our moral notions do *not* fit together into a comprehensive scheme.

Incommensurable values do not stand in the way of moral reasoning. They are part of what makes moral reasoning possible. Yet many philosophers hold that there is an irresolvable antinomy in any account of reason in ethics that allows for incommensurable values. On this basis, they reject the very idea of incommensurable values.[10]

Let us set out this argument against incommensurability in ethics. In ethics, as in science, theories or categories are incommensurable if they have no common core of meaning. Either there are incommensurable values or there are not. If there are, there cannot be rational choice between different moral outlooks. If there are not, then claiming that conflicts of value can rightly be settled in incompatible ways amounts to licensing inconsistent ethical beliefs. Either way, accepting that there are incommensurable values seems to destroy reason in ethics.

If moral notions are truly incommensurable, they can have no shared subject matter. Statements in which they occur cannot be mutually translated. As a consequence, they cannot contradict one another. It makes no more sense to say that judgements deploying incommensurable moral ideas are consistent or inconsistent with one another than it does to say that statements about the length of a piece of paper could be consistent or inconsistent with statements about its thickness. If there are incommensurables in ethics, they appear to have no logical relations with one another. Could there be a more formidable barrier to rationality?

If Homeric *arete* and Christian *agape* are mapped onto the same behaviour, they are incompatible. But what is the nature of their incompatibility? If the two ideas belong to radically different forms of life and conceptual frameworks, it is hard to see how they can contradict one another. If the categories they employ are incommensurate in their meaning, they can be neither consistent nor inconsistent, but merely different.

On the other hand, if they are not fully incommensurable, then judgements containing them will surely yield inconsistencies. A given human act cannot at the same time exemplify Homeric *arete* and Christian *agape*. If it is praised as embodying the one it must be condemned as expressing the other. What is meekness for St Paul is cowardice for Homer. Yet the same human behaviour cannot be both desirable and undesirable. That amounts to affirming both *p* and not-*p*, thereby violating the first prohibition of classical logic. To admit incommensurable values is therefore to tolerate contradictions.

That is, in brief, the argument that is commonly advanced against the claim that there are incommensurable values. The assumption underlying it is that if values are incommensurate they must belong to forms of life that have no categories or concepts in common. If this is so, judgements deploying values that are incommensurable cannot be mutually translatable. They are bound to be mutually unintelligible.

This common belief is not borne out in common life. We are constantly weighing and discussing ideas and values that are incommensurable. The idea that it is impossible to do so presupposes that such considerations must be components of different comprehensive conceptual frameworks. Yet the very idea of such a conceptual framework is suspect.[11]

Our various moral ideas do not belong to all-encompassing conceptual frameworks that are sealed off from one another.

The forms of life in which we find ourselves are not the windowless monads of Leibnizian metaphysics. They are more like prisms, in whose shifting lights we move. Few, if any of us are today radically situated subjects, embedded once and for all in a single way of life. Nearly all of us belong in several ways of life. It is the conflicts between (and within) ways of life that make us what we are.

Neither ethical life nor moral discourse is a closed system in whose 'categories', 'concepts', 'principles' or 'values' we are fixed. On the contrary, we move from one form of life to another, translating their key terms piecemeal, case-by-case, more or less freely. As we do this, we regularly perform feats of reasoning that theoretical ideals of rationality say are impossible.

In the ethical life with which we are familiar, we do not find ourselves trapped in a single, all-encompassing world-view. We find ourselves using a highly miscellaneous moral vocabulary. It is true that the terms of this vocabulary do not compose any kind of system. But that does not prevent us using them intelligently in our moral reasonings. Very different moral notions may not be literally translatable, but they can still be interpreted and well understood.

The seeming incompatibility of incommensurable values with reason in ethical life comes from thinking of language in a radically holistic way in which the meaning of every expression is linked with that of every other. In fact, no language could be seamless in the way suggested by talk of comprehensive conceptual schemes.[12]

As J.L. Austin notes in *A Plea for Excuses*:

> It seems to be too readily assumed that if we can only discover the true meanings of key terms, usually historic terms, that we use in some particular field (as, for example, 'right', 'good', and the rest in morals), then it must without question transpire that each will fit into some single, interlocking, conceptual scheme. Not only is there no reason to assume this, but all historical probability is against it, especially in the case of a language derived from various civilisations as ours is. We may cheerfully use, and with weight, terms which are not so much

head-on incompatible as simply *disparate*, which just do not
fit in or even on. Just as we cheerfully subscribe to, or have the
grace to be torn between, simply disparate ideals – why *must*
there be a conceivable amalgam, the Good Life for Man?[13]

Austin's argument provides a powerful rejoinder to the common view that recognizing incommensurable values means
embracing relativism. That might be so if such values came
packaged in tightly woven conceptual schemes. In truth, they
are only loosely connected with the forms of ethical life from
which they derive.

Relativism about values presupposes that forms of life can
be fully and finally individuated. That has never been true.
Ours has long been a civilization of traces and fragments. If
ways of life and moral languages were ever sharply delineated,
they are no longer. Late modern societies do not contain only
one moral language. Many of their members are morally mul-
tilingual.

It is part of the natural diversity of moral languages that
some should contain words for which others have no syno-
nyms. The ethical terms they use to distinguish virtues and
vices are too different in their meanings for a literal transla-
tion of them to be possible. But they can still be interpreted.
In societies like ours, this kind of interpretation goes on all
the time.

When people who stand in more than one way of life consider how their lives should go, they do what a theoretical
model of rationality says is impossible. They put values that
are incommensurable in the balance. By doing so they show
that, whatever its merits as a philosophical position, relativism has ceased to be a feasible stance in practice.

As a side-effect, conservatism has ceased to be a coherent
social philosophy. It is a conceit of conservative thought that
we can resolve moral dilemmas by pursuing the intimations of
tradition. Which tradition? It is often the rival intimations
of the different traditions to which we belong that engender
our ethical dilemmas.

When many ways of life interact, no tradition is self-
validating. The plurality of interpenetrating ways of life, among

which many people are able to move more or less freely according to their needs and purposes, has made the appeal to tradition an anachronism. The ethical pluralism of late modern societies has rendered conservatism incoherent.[14]

The claim that value-pluralism is a species of relativism depends on a radically holistic view of ethical life. That view is false to common experience. But relativism is not the only view with which value-pluralism is wrongly conflated. It is often confused with subjectivism.

The mirror-image of the view in which value-pluralism is conflated with relativism is the view that value-pluralism makes personal preferences the final authority in ethics. Where values are incommensurable, there is no way of resolving conflicts among them that all reasonable people are bound to accept. Since there can be no reason for any resolution over any other that everyone finds compelling, it seems to follow that what decides such questions can only be preferences – personal or collective. Preferences are desires, not beliefs; they express wants, not propositions. They can be neither true nor false. When they differ there can be no question of inconsistency. In that case, pluralism avoids relativism, but by collapsing into subjectivism.

On the other hand, if incommensurable values are *not* just personal preferences, then value-pluralism is just another name for inconsistency. If our judgements of value express our beliefs and not merely our preferences, we cannot (consistently) allow that incompatible judgements can both be right. Here we confront starkly the objection to all varieties of value-pluralism. Ideals of the good life are not merely different. They are rivals. This is not only because in most people's lives they tend to drive one another out. It is because they support incompatible judgements.

Contrary to this common objection, value-pluralism need not collapse into either relativism or subjectivism. Incommensurable ideals and values are often rivals; but the incompatibility of the judgements to which they give rise is practical, not logical. Conflicts among incommensurable values can sometimes be resolved only by expressing a preference; but our preferences about how we are to live are not brute wants.

They embody our beliefs about the experiences we will have if we live the way we want.

Our beliefs about the experiences we will have if we live the way we want may be true or false; but that does not mean there is one way that everyone is best off living. Ways of life may express false beliefs; but the relation of different ways of living to one another need not be that of truth with falsehood. It may be – and often is – one of pragmatic inconsistency. The appearance of contradiction comes from considering moral judgements outside of their social contexts. If we view moral judgements as accounts of the essential properties of human beings and their action, we slide inevitably into contradictions. After all, the same individual cannot have contradictory attributes. A human being can no more be cowardly and courageous, at one and the same time, than she can be tall and short. Nevertheless, she can easily be both in different contexts.

As Wittgenstein noted, we cannot disagree in our judgements unless there is much on which our judgements are agreed. We must have common practices if we are to make divergent judgements. Our practices are not, however, all of one piece. They are connected together, but in loose strands, not a tightly woven fabric. In consequence, the same behaviour can be judged differently in different practices. It is true that our judgements can be right or wrong only by reference to common practices; but different practices can reasonably be applied in different contexts.

When incommensurable values yield incompatible judgements, they are pragmatically inconsistent, not logically contradictory. A purely private value-judgement is no more imaginable than a private language. Even so, to say that applying different incommensurable values in different contexts is to contradict oneself is to beg the question that is at issue. As Wittgenstein put it: 'The civil status of a contradiction, or its status in civil life: there is the philosophical problem.'[15]

When moral practices are distant from one another in time or place, we have little difficulty in seeing that incompatible value-judgements need not be contradictory. It is easy to understand that polygamy might be right and monogamy wrong in the societies from which the Old Testament comes, while monogamy could be right and polygamy wrong in modern times.

Paradoxically, it is in our circumstances, in which many people belong to more than one moral practice, that we find difficulty in comprehending that the same behaviour can reasonably be evaluated differently in different contexts. We are used to the idea that moral judgements are applications of common practices. We have yet to adjust our thinking to the fact that we apply different common practices, and thereby honour different values, in different contexts of our lives.

There is nothing wrong in applying different values in different contexts. People who belong in more than one way of life can accept and apply different moral practices in different contexts of their lives. There is nothing contradictory in a person honouring rival values in different contexts of her life. The idea that doing so must be wrong or irrational is just a piece of Kantian detritus.

But how are we to decide what to do when our values have implications that cannot be reconciled? Compromise is not always possible. The contexts in which we make our judgements are not sealed off from one another. We can be in different social contexts at the same time. Indeed, in a society in which many people belong to more than one way of life, this is a common occurrence.

One cannot be, at one and the same time, a fully autonomous liberal individual and a dutifully obedient member of a traditional community. Not only may the demands of these ideals conflict; they support contradictory evaluations of the same behaviour. What shows up as personal autonomy in liberal morality may be disobedience or selfishness from the standpoint of traditional values. Say I am a second-generation Asian woman who must decide between an arranged marriage and a relationship based on personal choice. In that case an appeal to common practices will not suffice. I must decide which practice I accept. In such crucial cases, how am I to decide how to act?

This central issue in contemporary ethical theory may be explored in terms of a dialogue between Nietzsche and Mill.

Mill believed that human beings were convergent enough in their considered judgements of human well-being to come to a consensus on a single kind of life as best for the species. Mill's ethical theory is an account of those considered judgements, while his political theory is a wager that it is a liberal society that most effectively promotes the best kind of human life.

In opposition to Mill, Nietzsche believed that human beings differ too much for such a consensus on the good to be reasonably expected. What ethical inquiry revealed was not a consensus about the good but an ultimate plurality of perspectives on it. Nietzsche wrote in *Joyful Wisdom*: 'As the conditions for the maintenance of one community have been very different from those of other communities, there have been very different moralities; and in respect of the future . . . one can prophesy that there will still be very divergent moralities.'[16]

Nietzsche's writings contain nothing that might be called a coherent political theory. Still, one may say that for him different regimes advance different types and mixes of human flourishing. He is unclear whether different regimes can be ranked in desirability or worth. This is partly because he is unclear whether different ways of living can be compared in value. Sometimes he holds to a quasi-Aristotelian view in which they can be ranked in a hierarchy of worth; at others he adopts the pluralist view that this may be impossible. Where he is unequivocal is in his rejection of the possibility of species-wide convergence on the content of the good. It is this negative, sceptical side of his ethical theory that largely underpins his rejection of liberalism.

By the same token, Mill's liberalism stands on his account of the convergence of reasonable judgement regarding the content of human well-being. In his essay on *Utilitarianism*, he set out his revision of classical utilitarianism. Abandoning the Benthamite calculus in which all pleasures are commensurable, he proposed a theory of qualitative hedonism, according to which some pleasures are more valuable than others. He specified the 'higher', more valuable pleasures as those activities for which a competent judge, being familiar with a rel-

evant range of experiences, showed a decided preference. He
made the further claim that 'those who are equally acquainted
with, and equally capable of appreciating and enjoying, both,
do give a most marked preference to the manner of existence
which employs their higher faculties.'[17]

Mill was unclear whether the decided preferences of experienced judges were criteria for the higher pleasures, or
merely evidence for them. If the connection between the preferences of experienced judges and the higher pleasures is
criterial, experienced judges cannot be in error as to the content of the higher pleasures: whatever they prefer under appropriate conditions of informed choice *is* a higher pleasure.
If, on the other hand, the relationship between the preferences of experienced judges and the higher pleasures is evidential, then the higher pleasures form an independent subject
matter about which even experienced judges may be mistaken.

One flaw in Mill's account is his Victorian view of the higher
faculties. He takes for granted that the higher faculties are
intellectual and moral rather than physical and sensuous. In
identifying the higher human faculties with the intellect and
the moral emotions, he is in a long tradition, of which Aristotle is a notable early exemplar; but those who have cultivated
the pleasures of the body and the senses may differ from Aristotle and Mill on this point.

Mill's account of the higher pleasures is most at odds with
experience in its undefended assumption that informed judges
will prefer the same kinds of pleasures. Mill did not doubt
that those having knowledge of both would prefer reading
Plato to a day at the races, botanizing to a night of wine and
song. It is not clear how to square Mill's certainty on this point
with his repeated assertion that individual needs vary widely.
It is a matter of common experience that equally well-informed
people prefer different pleasures. This fact makes the evidential account of the relationship between informed judgement
and the higher pleasures hard to sustain.

As Mill presents it, the distinction between higher and lower
pleasures marks a ranking in value. Higher pleasures are worth
infinitely more than lower pleasures. This means that any
amount of a higher pleasure, however small, is worth more

than any amount of a lower pleasure, however large. Mill was able to accept this far-fetched view because, following Aristotle, he thought that when an informed judge is faced with a choice between two pleasures or activities he will (other things being equal) choose the one in which his higher faculties are most fully engaged. Again, like Aristotle, Mill took for granted that the higher faculties are intellectual and moral rather than physical and sensuous. Along with Aristotle and most other moral philosophers, he passed over the evident fact that developing some of our faculties means leaving others to wither.

Mill believed that the best life for each of us encompasses the all-round development of his or her individual powers. Such a view makes sense only if the growth of some of our powers does not stunt that of others. But if, for example, some kinds of creativity depend on lacks or defects in the personality, as when the work of a van Gogh or a Kafka expresses unresolved or repressed personal dilemmas; if self-knowledge can cause a person's creative powers to wither, as may happen in psychoanalysis; then an ideal in which all of our personal powers are maximally developed throughout our lives is unrealizable.[18]

Mill's ideal of personal development breaks down on the fact that different ways of living develop our different powers and faculties. In a parallel way, his revision of classical utilitarianism in terms of higher and lower pleasures runs aground on the incommensurable value of different pleasures. But this does not mean there can be no reason to prefer some pleasures over others. We can choose between pleasures only by expressing a preference among them; but our preferences can be better- or worse-founded. We can have reason to prefer different pleasures.

Our reasons for living any kind of life may come in the end from our goals; but our goals depend on our beliefs about the kind of life we want to live. They are laden with beliefs about the experiences their satisfaction will yield. Our goals may be chosen; the experiences they produce are not. When our beliefs are overturned by experience we have reason to change our goals. Even our preferences are not brute wants. They always embody beliefs that can be subjected to the test of experience. We can be in error about the life we want to live. When experience overthrows our beliefs about the lives we want to lead we have reason to alter our wants.

People have good reason to adopt a form of activity or a way of life if they have no false beliefs about it, if all their relevant beliefs about it are true and they have deliberated well about it. Of course this is a demanding set of conditions, rarely met in practice. It embodies the notion that the best life for anyone is the life he or she has most reason to live.

Between the criterial and the evidential views of the relations of informed choice with the higher pleasures, Mill is closer to the latter. As it stands, his ethical theory is a halfway house between classical utilitarianism and value-pluralism. The flaw in it is not that he takes the content of the higher pleasures to be (in part) a matter of discovery. It is that he takes for granted that the higher pleasures are the same for all, and fails to perceive that for any one of us they may be incompatible.

Mill's mistake was to think that the best life must be in its most central and important respects the same life for everybody. He was in no doubt that the best human life was that of autonomous individuals. At the same time, fearing a world that contained only autonomous individuals, he often praised diversity. Like liberal thought as a whole, Mill's thought is beset by these opposing impulses.

Mill was led to the mistaken belief that the best life is in its most essential respects the same for all because he held to a realist view of moral knowledge in which it had to be the same for all. In ethics, realism is the claim that our moral beliefs can be true or false. They have an independent subject matter in respect of which we can be mistaken. The good life may not be what we think it to be, or what we want it to be. It is something, at least partly independent of our beliefs and desires, that we can reasonably make an object of inquiry.

By contrast, subjectivism is the view that the good is finally what each of us wants. Since it makes no sense to assess preferences in terms of truth or falsehood, subjectivism denies that moral knowledge is even a possibility. As between realist theories in which ethical judgements have a subject matter independent of our beliefs and subjectivist theories in which they are nothing more than the expression of subjective preferences, Mill's position is closer to realism.[19]

Mill was bound to reject subjectivism, if only because he saw it – in the guise of what he often called intuitionism – as an obstacle to rational reform. Viewing our moral judgements as expressions of preference puts them beyond criticism. It thereby amounts to an endorsement of the status quo in society. Our preferences are brute facts about us. There can be no reason why they should be other than they are. Unless we are somehow misinformed in our factual beliefs, we cannot be mistaken about them. Moreover, since our preferences largely reflect the society in which we grow up, subjectivist ethical theories are in practice inherently conservative. For Mill, this was in itself enough to justify rejecting subjectivism and affirming the possibility of genuine knowledge of the good.

At the same time, Mill believed that the contents of moral knowledge were bound to be the same for all. In this he was faithful to the central Socratic tradition in European philosophy, and to the Enlightenment project of a universal rational morality which he had inherited from his classical utilitarian forebears. Mill favoured variety in forms of life; but he never doubted that the best life was the examined life – in modern terms, the life of autonomous individuals. That is why he insisted that the higher pleasures were the same for all.

As Mill understood them, the higher pleasures necessarily involve the development of the higher human powers, which – following the tradition established by Aristotle – he identified with the intellectual and moral powers. Mill thinks that the content of moral knowledge is bound to be essentially the same for all because, like Aristotle, he thinks that the best human life requires the all-round development of the higher human powers.

If, however, we recognize that different people may reasonably differ as to what they count as their higher powers, with some viewing their physical and sensual powers in this light; if we allow that, however they are viewed, developing some of our higher powers may mean stunting others; and if we accept that different people, and even the same person, may reasonably choose to develop different combinations of their higher powers – then Mill's reasons for thinking that the good life must in its essentials be the same for all fall away.

That does not mean Mill has to give up a realist account of the good. On the contrary, if we remove from his account the unwarranted assumption that the higher pleasures are the same for all, it exemplifies an account of the good that is modestly but genuinely realist. In this amended view, for each of us the good life is as much a matter of discovery as it is of subjective preference. Each of us can try out different modes of life in order to find out which of his higher powers he has most reason to develop. Each of us may be in error as to the good life, without their being a truth about it that is the same for all.

Even in this amended form, Mill's account embodies the mistaken view that there must be one kind of life that is best for each of us. It is this view that Nietzsche rightly rejected, albeit intermittently and none too clearly, when he claimed that all valuation is perspectival. In a perspectivist ethical theory, all knowledge of the good is from a particular standpoint. It expresses particular human interests, as they are embodied in specific historical and social contexts. There can be no view of the good that transcends all perspectives. Nietzsche's perspectival account of our knowledge of the good implies that, not only for different people but even for the same person, there may be no one form of life that is best. In both cases the reason is the same. Views of the good express particular human interests, and for different people and even the same person these interests are often in conflict.

A perspectivist view of ethical knowledge entails that there need be no one view of the good that is better than all others. It does not mean there are not better and worse views of the good. Moral knowledge can be improved by filtering out distortions in our perspectives on the good. Because they incorporate a wider range of evidences and a deeper understanding of human experience, some perspectives are better than others. A perspectival account does not ensure convergence in our view of the good, but it does allow for moral learning.

Nietzsche's perspectival account of the good is a version of irrealism.[20] In ethics, irrealism is the claim that we can identify errors without there being any single reality that our ethical beliefs track. Each may be in error as to the good life, without it being true that there must be one life that is best for him. Indeed, if some of our higher pleasures cannot be combined and some combinations of them cannot be compared in value, there cannot be such a life. I can be mistaken in my beliefs about the kind of life I want to lead without it being true that there is only one kind of life that is best for me, or that I *really* want to lead.

So long as I can correct my false beliefs about it, the good life remains an object of inquiry for me. True, there are no fixed rules for determining when our ethical beliefs are in error. In this, however, ethics is no different from science. That does not mean that every question about the good life has one right answer. There can be many answers that are wrong and many that are right. In this, ethics resembles art.

From one standpoint, irrealism in ethics is closer to the realist assertion of the objectivity of value-judgement than it is to any of the standard varieties of scepticism, relativism and subjectivism. For it affirms that the content of the good life depends not on our beliefs and opinions, our preferences or decisions, but on experience. From another point of view, irrealism means giving up a traditional ideal of truth in ethics. Though we can be in error about how we want to live, there need be no one truth about the best life. There are many things the good life is not, but no one thing it is bound to be.

An irrealist account of ethics differs from theories that try to preserve the objectivity of value-judgements by invoking the public character of our moral practices. Rightly, these 'internal realist' theories note that moral judgements are not mere expressions of preference and sentiment. When we judge something to be cruel or unfair, we apply a common language and some common standards. This is true no less when we disagree in our judgements than when we agree. For, as I have noted, disagreement is possible only insofar as we have some judgements in common.[21]

Internal realism is right that judgements of value require common practices. Where it goes astray is in claiming that the publicness of moral practices can establish the objectivity of ethical judgements. What theories of internal realism neglect is that many people belong to rival moral practices, each of which carries with it a different view of moral reality. True, within each moral practice judgements of truth and falsity can be made; but different practices entail incompatible judgements. The question that must be answered by people who belong to rival practices is not what view of the good their practices entail. It is which practice, if any, to follow.

Despite its name, internal realism is a species of conventionalism. It makes truth in ethics depend – in the last analysis – on convention. By contrast, irrealism holds that questions of value are answered at the bar of experience. The beliefs that our moral practices express are not immune to revision. They and the practices that go with them are rightly abandoned when experience tells against them. The hard core of ethical life is found in those experiences that cannot be altered by changing our beliefs about them. Our moral beliefs are corrigible inasmuch as they can be undermined by those experiences. It is not through our practices and conventions that judgements of value have objectivity. It is by tracking experience; but experience does not support a single view of the good. In an irrealist view, we can be in error about the good life, but not all questions about the good have one true answer.

Value-pluralism and an irrealist view of the good go together. There is sometimes no truth of the matter about how we are to live. The truth of the matter is in the dilemma. Dilemmas of this kind may arise when we belong to rival moral practices, which embody different views of the good. (Of course they can arise equally within a single moral practice and its conception of the good.) We cannot simply apply our moral practices, for they are themselves at odds. We must decide how we are to live.

In such cases, the choices we are called upon to make are so fundamental and comprehensive in their implications for our lives that we know that we will be much altered by them. Yet there may remain a deep uncertainty about their effects on us. Without knowing the experiences which will thereby result, we are called to choose the kind of life we mean to have. Such radical choices occur as crises in ethical life, not as normal episodes within it. Yet, as more people come to belong to several ways of life, choices of this far-reaching kind tend to become more frequent. People whose identities are shaped by several ways of life must attempt to resolve their conflicting demands. They do so by recurrent choices, some of which will be radical choices of the kind I have mentioned. As they make these choices, people shape new identities for themselves, often in ways they could not have foreseen.

The idea of self-creation through choice-making should not be confused with the subjectivist notion of the primacy of personal preferences. The identities that human subjects choose for themselves are responses to dilemmas that are unchosen. Self-creation is never *ex nihilo*. Even our most radical choices are not the expression of purely subjective preferences.

There is surely a sense in which our most radical dilemmas can be resolved only by making a decision. The contexts in which we make such decisions are not chosen, however, but fated. Moreover, though what such a person confronts is a choice of the self she means to be, the result of her choice may well be one she would not have chosen.

Someone whose identity has been shaped by forms of life that have come to make irreconcilable demands on him can settle his dilemma only by an act of will. But neither the circumstances that give rise to his dilemma nor the experiences that result from his choice are determined by what he wills. As different human subjects resolve such dilemmas in different ways, new identities and values are shaped from those that have been inherited from the past.

Nietzsche perceived that there will always be many moralities. The diversity of histories and circumstances, the varieties of temperament and human needs ensure that in the future, as in the past, there will be many different perspectives on the good. That does not mean one perspective is as good as any other. (Nietzsche plainly believed that his perspective on the good was superior to those of Pascal and Schopenhauer, say.) It means there need not be any perspective on the good that is better than all others. Indeed, if some kinds of good life are incommensurate in value, as Nietzsche sometimes suggests, there cannot be such a perspective.

Nietzsche was right to reject Mill's Enlightenment faith that human beings are bound to converge in their judgements regarding the good. His mistake was to deny that there are evils that can prevent practically anyone from having a good life.

The claim that there are generically human evils does not rest finally on a consensus of belief. It rests on the fact that the experiences to which these evils give rise are much the same for all human beings, whatever their ethical beliefs may be. The constancy with which these experiences are found, across remote cultures and distant epochs, reflects a constancy in human nature, not an agreement in opinions. Like other animals, humans have a stock of needs that does not change much, and which constrains the forms of life in which they can thrive. Whenever the thwarting of a generically human need renders a worthwhile life unattainable, there is a universal evil.

There can be no definitive list of the conditions that endanger a worthwhile human life. Even so, to be tortured, or forced to witness the torture of loved ones or compatriots; to be separated from one's friends, family or country; to be subjected to humiliation or persecution, or threatened with genocide; to be locked in poverty or avoidable ill-health – these are great evils for all who suffer them. Insofar as a conception of the good does not encompass these experiences, it is defective, even delusive.

Relativists, subjectivists and sceptics who think a shift in moral practices or beliefs could alter our judgement of these universal evils have forgotten a vital Hobbesian truth. Altering our beliefs about ourselves does not change our needs. Human beings are not made of their opinions. Every human being is at risk from evils that can make any kind of good life difficult, or impossible.

Yet such universal evils do not ground a universal minimum morality. When faced with conflicts among them, different individuals and ways of life can reasonably make incompatible choices. Differing ways of life come partly from divergent settlements among universal evils. The content of the universal evils to which human life is subject is a matter of knowledge, of true belief founded on experience; but rational inquiry does not yield a single answer as to which we are to choose when universal evils collide.

More, universal evils do not always override particular loyalties. There is nothing unreasonable in putting the claims of one's way of life over those of universal values. One who fights against hopeless odds to preserve his way of life, or who chooses death rather than accept its extinction, incurs universal evils; but what he does is not necessarily wrong. Conflicts between universal values and the claims of particular ways of life engender dilemmas that are as common, and sometimes as intractable, as those that arise when we must choose among universal evils. In both cases, no one settlement of the conflict we face is uniquely right, or reasonable; but some can be better than others.

To affirm the reality of universal human goods and evils is not to endorse a universal morality, such as many liberal thinkers have attempted to defend. Universal values are compatible with many moralities, including liberalism as it has been understood by recent philosophers who take their cue from Locke or Kant; but they underdetermine them all. There is no one regime that can reasonably be imposed on all. Even minimal standards can be met in different ways. Minimally legitimate regimes need not, and often do not, protect the same basic rights. Like the universal evils they are framed to prevent, basic rights conflict with one another. Such conflicts can rightly be settled in a variety of ways.

Different regimes need not be approximations to any ideal type. Indeed they cannot be. Nor are different regimes fated to be antagonists. As between two highly legitimate regimes which resolve conflicts of rights or values in incompatible ways, the one need neither be better or worse than the other, nor roughly as good. They may simply be different. So may be two minimally legitimate regimes which resolve conflicts between and within the most basic rights in different ways.

No regime can truly claim to embody the best settlement of conflicts among universal values. Disputes about which regime is everywhere best are without sense. The diversity of regimes is like the diversity of goods. It is not a mark of any lack in human life. It is a sign of the abundance of good lives that human beings can live.

One of the paradoxes that comes with accepting that there are incommensurable values is that tragic conflicts of value can sometimes melt away. If there are many incommensurable ways in which humans can flourish, choices among them need not be tragic. Different regimes and ways of life can cease to be antagonists and become alternatives. When this happens, value-pluralism as a theory of ethics points towards *modus vivendi* as a political ideal.

3

Rival Freedoms

A contemporary orthodoxy asserts that conflicts of value are what make liberal regimes legitimate. Liberal regimes enable people whose views of the good life are at odds to live together on terms they can all accept as fair. They can agree on these principles and how they are to be applied in particular cases despite disagreeing in their conceptions of the good. As John Rawls puts it, stating this orthodoxy canonically: ' . . . liberal principles can be applied following the usual guidelines of public inquiry and rules for assessing evidence. . . . Hence applying liberal principles has a certain simplicity.'[1]

If, however, the freedoms that liberal principles enjoin can be rivals; if such conflicts can be resolved only by invoking judgements of the good on which reasonable people may differ; if, in the absence of such judgements, liberal principles are devoid of content; if, that is to say, applying liberal principles necessarily involves resolving conflicts among incommensurable values – then liberal principles have nothing of the simplicity of which Rawls speaks. Liberal regimes are no different from others in having to make choices between rival freedoms; but liberal principles cannot tell them how to make them.

The ruling orthodoxy in contemporary political philosophy understands liberalism as a prescription, universal in authority and application, for an ideal regime; but when the principles of that regime are subject to scrutiny they are found to harbour conflicts of value which they cannot resolve. The account of liberalism as a system of universal principles breaks down on conflicts of value for which there is no single solution. In consequence, we should give up the view of the liberal project as a prescription for an ideal regime and adopt instead a conception in which the pursuit of *modus vivendi* among incommensurable and conflicting values is central.

That will be my argument. Let us consider Rawls's celebrated theory of justice as fairness, in particular his account of basic liberties. In *A Theory of Justice*, Rawls follows a long liberal tradition by defending a principle giving priority to liberty over other values. He claims that giving priority to liberty does not require making choices among rival freedoms or making controversial judgements about the worth of these freedoms. He contends that justice demands that each person have the greatest liberty that is compatible with other people having the same liberty. This 'Greatest Equal Liberty Principle' requires that each person have the most extensive liberty, subject to others having the same, and enjoins that liberty should be restricted only for the sake of liberty.[2]

Rawls's principle has a distinguished liberal pedigree. Versions of it can be found in many liberal thinkers, including Kant and Hayek, Henry Sidgwick and Herbert Spencer, among others. Nevertheless, as one of this century's most penetrating liberal philosophers demonstrated, Rawls's principle is fundamentally flawed. In an incisive critique,[3] Herbert Hart showed that Rawls's Greatest Equal Liberty Principle suffers from a disabling indeterminacy.

Judgements of the greatest liberty are not free-standing. They depend on assessments of the relative importance of the human interests that different liberties protect. Claims about the greatest liberty cannot be value-free. They vary along with differing views of human interests. Rawls writes as if any reasonable person can know what the greatest liberty is. The truth is that it is indeterminate to the last degree.

Our judgements of greater and lesser liberty are judgements of the worth of the liberties that are at stake. This is a necessary truth which applies in all but a few limiting cases. If we differ in our views of what is humanly worthwhile, we will differ in our judgements of what constitutes the greatest liberty. Our views of what counts as the greatest liberty are applications of our view of human interests. Liberal precepts such as Rawls's avoid indeterminacy only by evaluating the interests that different combinations of liberties affect. They do so by deploying conceptions of the good life that specify some interests as weighty and ranking them in order of importance. Liberty cannot be restricted only for the sake of liberty. We cannot prevent conceptions of the good entering into the judgements we make when we apply liberal principles giving priority to liberty. The idea of the greatest liberty has a definite content only insofar as we apply our view of the good. Because our judgements about liberty apply our conceptions of the good, the priority of liberty over other values that is so dear to Rawls and other liberals of his school cannot be sustained.

Hart gives several examples of the indeterminacy of the greatest liberty. He cites rules of order in debate, which restrict the liberty to speak as we please. We have rules of order in debate so that the exchange of arguments and the pursuit of truth can be facilitated. We have these rules not so that debaters can exercise the maximum freedom to speak (if we can attach any meaning to such a strange notion), but in order better to achieve the purposes of debate.

Hart's aim in citing this example is to show that Rawls's Greatest Equal Liberty Principle, along with other similar liberal precepts, suffers from a damaging indeterminacy. Unless they are informed by some view of human interests, such venerable liberal principles cannot be applied. Indeed, in the absence of some such view, they are practically devoid of content.

Hart's critique of Rawls poses a more fundamental challenge to liberalism perhaps than he realized. If the ideal of the most extensive liberty acquires a definite content only by invoking specific conceptions of the good, liberal regimes cannot be defended on the ground that they contain a system of liberties that all reasonable people must accept. Every liberal regime protects a particular combination of liberties regarding which reasonable people may differ.

Like non-liberal regimes, liberal regimes embody specific conceptions of the good life. The liberties they protect can be justified only in terms of those conceptions. Of course no liberal regime embodies a single conception of the good. All embody a local settlement of the claims of rival ideals. The freedoms that any liberal regime protects are parts of this settlement.

However liberal, no regime can meet fully the demands of all important liberties. The freedoms that are protected in actually existing liberal regimes are not applications of any principle about the priority of liberty. They are compromises among rival views of the good – and between the rival claims each of these views can make.

Liberal regimes are states in which the claims of rival freedoms are negotiated openly. The notion of an ideal liberal regime, in which the claims of all important liberties have been reconciled to everyone's satisfaction, is incoherent. In having to reconcile the demands of incompatible liberties, liberal regimes are no different from others. Whether they admit it or not, liberal regimes – like all others – are enmeshed in conflicts of value.

It is because he grasped that Hart's critique of the Greatest Equal Liberty Principle could be the undoing of his ideal of the liberal state that Rawls developed his account of the basic liberties. In *A Theory of Justice*, Rawls enumerated the basic liberties as follows: 'political liberty (the right to vote and be eligible for public office), together with freedom of speech and assembly; liberty of conscience and freedom of thought; freedom of the person along with the right to hold (personal) property; and freedom from arbitrary arrest and seizure as defined by the concept of the rule of law'.[4]

Hart's argument demonstrated that no list of the basic liberties can be justified on the ground that it promotes the most extensive liberty. In *Political Liberalism* Rawls replaces the idea of the most extensive system of liberty with an account of the basic liberties. In that work, the sketch of basic liberties contained in *A Theory of Justice* is filled out so that the idea of the greatest liberty can be dispensed with; but the conflict of liberties is not thereby avoided.

It was the indeterminacy of Rawls's principle, pointed out by Hart, that moved him to develop his account of the basic liberties. As he has written, it was 'the indeterminate and unguided balancing problems we had hoped to avoid by a suitably circumscribed notion of priority'[5] which motivated the development of the theory of basic liberties.

The resulting theory is no more satisfactory than the initial principle. It excludes from the category of basic liberties freedoms that many liberals consider vitally important. All that Rawls has done is to move from indeterminacy to arbitrariness in his choice of the freedoms that liberal principles protect.

The absence of important liberal freedoms from Rawls's list of basic liberties is not inadvertent. It flows from an insuperable difficulty in his theory. The choice of some liberties as basic presupposes an evaluation of the human interests they protect. People with differing conceptions of human interests, or who differ in the importance they give to the interests they agree in recognizing, will make different judgements as to which liberties are basic.

When Rawls moves from the Greatest Equal Liberty Principle to his list of basic liberties he diminishes the indeterminacy of the liberty his principles protect; but in precisely the same degree he increases the conflicts of value which they engender. As a result, Rawls's liberal principles waver incessantly between the Scylla of indeterminacy and the Charybdis of incommensurability.

Rawls claims that applying liberal principles 'has a certain simplicity'. Nothing is needed to apply them, he tells us, other than 'the usual guidelines for public inquiry and rules for assessing evidence'. At the same time, he insists that liberal principles must be accepted by all reasonable people. When the claims of competing liberties need to be reconciled, these requirements are incompatible.

The idea that applying 'liberal principles' is an easy matter is all of a piece with the notion that rules of justice have a single meaning. But if applying any rule involves judgement, and people with different views of the good make different judgements when they apply the same rule, then conflicting views of the good will reappear in incompatible applications of the same 'liberal principles'.

Rawls's account of the basic liberties is meant to avoid the indeterminacy that afflicts discourse regarding the greatest liberty. Yet recasting his theory in terms of rules prescribing basic liberties does not overcome his difficulty. For these rules are themselves liable to incompatible interpretations. This is in conformity with Wittgenstein's scepticism regarding formalist accounts of what it is to follow a rule.[6]

Following a rule offers no escape from the uncertainties and creativity of human judgement. In this respect the liberal principles Rawls invokes are no different from any other rules. They do not apply themselves. They are applied by human beings, with all the uncertainty that entails.

Rawls's system is an attempt to evade the difficulties of political judgement by giving liberal principles the certainty of law. But that certainty is delusive. Like any other human practice, law requires making decisions. Laws conflict, and the same law can be given incompatible interpretations.

If all that was at issue was some indeterminacy in Rawls's principles, and consequently a few hard cases in applying them, nothing much would follow. Indeterminacies and hard cases are found in every area of thought and practice. What is disabling to Rawls's enterprise is not primarily any indeterminacy in his principles. It is that incompatible applications of his principles can be justified by different conceptions of the good.

Different judgements about what Rawls's principles mean in particular cases arise from different judgements about human interests. As a consequence, the same principles have quite different implications depending on the moral outlooks of those who apply them. This is a calamitous result for Rawls, since it destroys the possibility of a strictly political liberalism which is independent of any substantive conception of the good.

The dependency of Rawls's principles on substantive judgements of the good goes to the heart of the conception of liberalism as a theory of an ideal regime.[7] His theory is designed to exclude incommensurable values from political philosophy. If the principles that define an ideal regime cannot be applied without settling conflicts among values that are incommensurable, an ideal regime is not even conceivable. Political liberalism claims to be based on the fact of reasonable pluralism; but the principles of justice in which it consists are supposed to be insulated from radical choices among incommensurables.[8] Rawlsian justice can have no place for radical choice among conflicting values. If, as is demonstrably the case, such radical choices are necessary when we attempt to apply Rawls's principles, his theory is compromised fatally.

That Rawls's theory is designed to relieve liberal principles from having to resolve conflicts of value is clear from his account of the basic liberties. The requirement that basic liberties dovetail into an harmonious system is not inadvertent. As I note later in this chapter, it is partly an unreflective application of the local conventions of American jurisprudence. More fundamentally, it is an essential move in an argument designed to protect liberal principles from the pluralism to which they are supposed to be a response.

The list of basic liberties that Rawls advances is rather parsimonious. It offers few hostages to fortune. After all, it was designed to avoid the indeterminacy that plagued the Greatest Equal Liberty Principle. Inasmuch as it succeeds in escaping vagueness, however, it cannot avoid conflicts among the liberties that it singles out as basic.

Rawls is careful not to deny that such conflicts occur. He writes:

> Since the various basic liberties are bound to conflict with one another, the institutional rules which define these liberties must be adjusted so that they fit into a coherent scheme of liberties. The priority of liberty implies in practice that a basic liberty can be limited or denied solely for the sake of one or more other basic liberties. . . . Since the basic liberties may be limited when they clash with one another, none of these liberties is absolute; nor is it a requirement that, in the finally adjusted scheme, all the basic liberties are to be equally provided for
> . . . .

Having apparently acknowledged that basic liberties may conflict, Rawls goes on to distinguish between the regulation of basic liberties and their restriction. 'The priority of these liberties is not infringed when they are regulated, as they must be, in order to be combined into one scheme. So long as what I shall call "the central range of application" of the basic liberties is provided for, the principles of justice are fulfilled.' Armed with this distinction, Rawls concludes: ' . . . under reasonably favorable conditions, there is a practicable scheme of liberties that can be instituted in which the central range of each liberty is protected.'[9]

The proposal that the 'central range' of basic liberties be 'adjusted' and 'regulated' so as to circumvent conflicts between them does little justice to the difficulty of the questions that arise in such cases. Vitally important liberties do not dovetail into a single, harmonious pattern. They are sites of conflicts of value. The suggestion that such conflicts can be resolved by 'adjusting' the basic liberties is unpersuasive. Indeed it is not much more than a sleight of hand.

It is true that basic liberties, along with the other primary goods that are recognized in Rawls's theory, may reinforce one another. As an example, the basic liberty of expression that is embodied in a free press can protect other basic liberties. If they are likely to be investigated and publicized by free media, violations of basic liberties other than those involved in free expression may be less likely to occur. Again, people are less likely to be denied a decent range of opportunities in social and economic life if they possess effective political rights. Equally, people who are assured of basic rights to welfare and education are less likely to be subject to systematic violation of their civil and political rights.

Even so, there is nothing that ensures this benign result.[10] If freedom of speech clashes with freedom from racist abuse; if the freedom from invasion of privacy claimed by public figures and private citizens collides with the freedom of expression required by investigative journalists; if the freedoms of association and conscience claimed by Catholics, Muslims and others in setting up schools in which gay teachers are not hired are incompatible with the freedom of gays from homophobic discrimination in employment; if freedom to proselytize endangers the freedom to practise one's religion without fear of persecution – then there is a genuine conflict of liberties which cannot be conjured away by 'adjusting' or 'regulating' them. In fact, conflicts among basic liberties are not anomalies, or rare hard cases. They are endemic in law and politics.

As a paradigm case of conflict involving basic liberties, consider freedom of speech. (In what follows I follow Rawls in confining discussion to what may be reasonably considered to be *political* speech; but nothing turns on this.) For Rawls, free speech is one element in a system of dovetailing liberties. The 'central range of application' of freedom of speech dovetails into the system of basic liberties as a whole. Using a term borrowed from Leibniz, we may say that Rawls views the basic liberties as a compossible set. Basic liberties cannot be incompatible with one another; within their central range of application they are necessarily harmonious: ' . . . the basic liberties not only limit one another; but they are also self-limiting.'[11] It follows (for Rawls) that freedom of speech can never conflict with another basic liberty.

Rawls tells us that the 'central range of application' of free speech requires that there be no prior restraints on freedom of the press, no offence of seditious libel, and that the advocacy of subversive and revolutionary doctrines be fully protected. Let us grant these claims. But cannot protecting a freedom of speech that comes clearly within this central range conflict with other basic liberties? And with weighty public interests? When free speech collides with other liberties, or with a weighty public interest, is it always wrong to restrict it? Let us be more specific. May not freedom of (political) speech be rightly curbed when it is used to promote racism?

It is a salient fact that Britain and most other European countries have legislated against racist speech. So has Canada. In none of these cases can the law be described as merely regulating freedom of speech. Curbs on racist speech do not regulate speech. They curb it. In the great majority of constitutional democracies, speech is restrained in this way.

Curiously, Rawls fails to mention this fact. This is surprising, since he holds that his theory of justice is founded in the traditions and values of constitutional democracies, not on those only of the United States. Yet there is a good deal more to Rawls's neglect than American parochialism.

Rawls cannot maintain that the curbs on racist speech that are found in most liberal democracies are not genuine restraints on free speech. After all, this is amply evident from the constitutional history of the United States, in which attempts to curb racist speech have been repeatedly struck down as restraints of liberty. American judges have regularly defeated attempts to prohibit racist speech because they understand that such bans curb speech rather than merely contouring it.

The difference of judgement between American judges and European legislators is not about whether banning racist speech is a curb on freedom of expression. On that they are agreed. It is about whether such a curb can be justified. European legislators have judged that curbs on racist speech may protect basic liberties (even as they restrict them). They may protect the political liberties of minorities, including liberty of speech itself.

If, following the example of the American judiciary, we accept that curbs on racist speech are not mere contourings of freedom of expression but instead restraints on it, we are compelled to confront the awkward fact that basic liberties make conflicting demands. They do so not just at the margin, or in a few hard cases, but in virtue of their core content, and quite frequently.

One basic liberty clashes with another, or with the same basic liberty, or with important social values that are not basic liberties. The distinction between basic liberties and other values is not categorical. It is breached whenever one liberty clashes with another. In order to resolve conflicts between basic liberties we must assess which liberty is most important. To do that we must consider their impact on society.

The different responses of European legislators and American judges to the issues posed by racist speech have a number of sources. Among them are differing assessments of the dangers to individual liberty of legal restraint of free expression and divergent evaluations of the importance of social cohesion in promoting individual well-being. These differences are not unconnected. They express different histories, conceptions of government and ideals of the good life.

In assessing the social effects of rival liberties we are once again enmeshed in conflicts of value. Such cases of conflicting values are not uncommon. They recur whenever liberal ideals are honoured. Liberal principles give little guidance in resolving them.[12]

There are several ways in which vitally important liberal freedoms may be rivals. They may make incompatible demands on the same domain of options. Where this happens, the exercise of one freedom is in itself a violation of another. If freedom of association includes the freedom to sack teachers because they are gay, and if freedom from homophobic discrimination includes the prohibition of such sackings, the two freedoms are rivals in that they cannot logically be exercised together.

Such freedoms cannot be combined, not merely because in practice they are mutually exclusive alternatives, but because they embody opposed ideals. There is a contradiction in the notion that freedom of racist expression and freedom from racist abuse can both be fully protected. Protecting people from racist abuse entails curbing racist speech. The two freedoms are logically incompatible.

At the same time, their consequences and effects on liberal institutions may be very different. Being logically incompatible is only the simplest way in which vital liberal freedoms may be rivals. They can also undermine one another through their practical effects and through the tendency of some of their uses to weaken or subvert liberal regimes. Here vital freedoms are rivals not because they exclude one another by necessity but because of their consequences.

European (and American) history suggests that a society in which racist speech is free easily becomes one in which the speech of racial minorities is unfree. In that case, curbing the freedom of speech of racists may be justified on the ground that it protects the freedom of speech of racial minorities.

These considerations tell heavily in favour of curbs on racist speech. They do not show that liberal regimes everywhere must contain such curbs. A society in which racism was un-

known – if there were such a society – might be one in which
freedom of racist expression could be safely protected. Equally,
the risk of protecting racist speech could be worth taking if it
helped to establish a regime of free expression where none
had hitherto existed.

I am not convinced that these possibilities are realistic. Even
so, the burden of my argument is not that every liberal regime
is bound to ban racist speech. On the contrary, it is that even
on this fundamental matter liberal regimes may rightly differ.

When freedom of expression collides with other important
freedoms, or with other goods, it engenders a conflict about
whose solution reasonable people may differ. Different regimes of free expression may be neither better nor worse than
one another, nor roughly the same in value. They may simply
be different, in that they embody incompatible solutions of
conflicts among incommensurable values.

When freedom of racist speech and freedom from racist
abuse are rivals, liberal principles cannot tell us which is to be
protected. To determine that, we must apply our conception
of the good society to the specific historical circumstances of
particular regimes. When we do so, we find that many
freedoms which liberal principles specify as basic are – in logic,
or in fact – rivals.

This is *not* to say that, when circumstances prevent the full
implementation of the system of basic liberties, Rawls must
fall back on a second-best solution. That is what Rawls himself claims in his account of 'partial compliance' with the principles of justice. Rather, what the example of racist speech
shows is that full compliance – protecting all the basic liberties – is an impossibility. It is not because he has to fall back
on second-best solutions that Rawls's theory fails. It is because his account of the best solution is incoherent. It is not
the imperfections of human beings that make Rawls's ideal
regime unattainable. It is because a regime in which all basic
liberties are fully protected is not even conceivable.

Rawls assumes that basic liberties form what he calls a 'coherent scheme'. He makes this assumption because he takes
for granted that fundamental rights cannot make incompatible demands. Basic rights are to be 'regulated', 'adjusted' or

'contoured' so as to avoid conflicting with one another. Rights cannot then clash with rights; but it is recognized that their exercise can endanger other goods. When that happens there is nothing to be done. If freedom of speech is used to foment racism, the right of free speech must nevertheless be upheld, otherwise the priority of rights over other values is compromised.

These are not views for which Rawls offers much argument. They are elements of an American constitutional tradition for which he appears to see little need to argue. In his *Collected Papers*, Rawls reaffirms that his theory of justice 'is formulated so far as possible solely in terms of certain fundamental intuitive ideas viewed as implicit in the public culture of a democratic society'.[13] Among those ideas Rawls appears to include the notion that basic liberties or rights cannot make genuinely conflicting demands.

Yet this is not a notion accepted by many constitutional democracies. When rights clash with each other or within themselves, many liberal states – such as Canada and most European states – do not respond by seeking to conjure away these conflicts by 'adjusting' or 'regulating' their 'central range of application'. They conclude that some demands of rights override or defeat others and seek reasons of public interest to decide the issue at hand. Implicit in this procedure is the recognition that when rights clash their conflict can be rightly settled in different ways.

It is no accident that conflict among basic liberties is evaded in Rawls's work. Rawls's theory of basic liberties gives no account of how such conflicts are to be settled because it is designed to suppress them. The theory of basic liberties was developed to circumvent the necessity of making controversial judgements about the greatest liberty. The necessity was not avoided but instead obscured.

The stipulation that basic liberties compose a compossible set is not an incidental defect in Rawlsian liberalism. It is essential to the enterprise of a liberal philosophy of right. Only if basic rights or liberties cannot make incompatible demands can justice be insulated from conflicts of value.

If basic liberties clash, there is no way of avoiding judgements of importance among the human interests they protect. Manifestly, such judgements will vary with different conceptions of the good. The argument of which among a set of rival liberties is to be protected, and in what degree, is then inescapably an argument about the good. At that point, conflicts of value re-emerge at the core of political philosophy, and the Rawlsian enterprise faces ruin.

Once it is allowed that important liberties may be rivals, we are not far from accepting that their conflicts have no solutions which are acceptable to all reasonable persons. In that case, different mixes of liberties may be right in different societies. Even in a single society, people may reasonably differ as to how the claims of rival freedoms, or rival components of the same freedom, are best reconciled.

At this point the ramshackle edifice of the basic liberties collapses. As a result, liberal regimes can no longer be marked off from all others by protecting any particular combination of liberties. All regimes embody particular settlements among rival liberties.

That is a result which illustrates the accuracy of Isaiah Berlin's observation, when he wrote:

> If the claims of two (or more than two) types of liberty prove incompatible in a particular case, and if this is an instance of the clash of values at once absolute and incommensurable, it is better to face this intellectually uncomfortable fact than to ignore it, or automatically attribute it to some deficiency on our part which could be eliminated by an increase in skill or knowledge; or, what is worse still, suppress one of the competing values altogether by pretending it is identical with its rival – and so end by distorting both.[14]

Conflicting liberties are not peculiar to Rawlsian liberalism. All liberal philosophies that aim to define an ideal regime are beset by them. They do not come only from indeterminacies in the idea of maximal liberty. Liberal philosophies that have no truck with ideals of maximum liberty or with maximizing any value are undone by them.

Despite its fastidious aversion to maximization,[15] Robert

Nozick's theory of side-constraints founders on precisely these conflicts. Side-constraints are what Kantian thinkers call fundamental rights. They are meant to set up impassable barriers against anyone – governments or private agencies – treating people merely as resources. In Nozick's account side-constraints are limits on action of enormous weight. That much is clear.

The contents of side-constraints are harder to specify. No list is given of them. Nozick does not tell us whether there is only one side-constraint or many. We do not know if all rights are branches of a single tree, or independent growths from separate roots. For my present argument these omissions do not matter. Any side-constraint defeats the claims of any other value. When they come into conflict with any other moral consideration, Nozick's side-constraints have infinite weight. (Nozick has a cryptic aside suggesting that he would entertain violations of side-constraints in order to forestall moral catastrophes; but he fails to specify what might count as such a catastrophe.[16])

Still, Nozick's side-constraints cannot all be *equally* weighty. Side-constraints may have an infinite weight when they conflict with other values, but when they conflict *with each other* some must be weightier than others. This must be so, whether there is only one fundamental side-constraint or a number of independently derived side-constraints on how people may rightly be treated.

Suppose the only way I can prevent someone from being murdered is by borrowing an umbrella against someone else's will. Here a side-constraint of one kind (against violating property rights) competes with another (against violating the right to life); but side-constraints of the same kind may equally be rivals. I may borrow the same umbrella against its owner's will in order to prevent someone's life-savings being stolen. Either way, one side-constraint is overridden by another.

If it is allowed that side-constraints can be more or less weighty, it is impossible to avoid the implication that less weighty rights-violations may sometimes be permissible, even required, if they are necessary in order to prevent weightier violations of other rights or of the same right. Yet there is nothing in Nozick's account about how conflicts between side-constraints of differing weight are to be resolved. (It may be worth noting that where a side-constraint is justifiably over-ridden, it does not thereby cease to exist. It may trigger a subsequent claim for compensation or restitution.)

It is not hard to account for this lacuna. Conflicts among rights cannot be resolved without invoking the values that inform the system of rights as a whole. We cannot account for differences in severity among rights-violations without bringing into account the various interests such violations harm.

It is not impossibly hard to see why borrowing someone's umbrella, even against his will, is a lesser rights-violation than murdering him. The damage done to anyone by being murdered is vastly worse than that which is inflicted by the temporary loss of an umbrella. We cannot judge the severity of rights-violations without such knowledge of the relative importance of ordinary human interests.

Unless we know the interests they protect, rights lack content. When we know these interests, we find that rights, even a single right, may make incompatible demands. Then we have no alternative to choosing between them.

It is not because we are committed to maximizing anything that we are forced to choose which of the demands of rights we are going to respect. We are compelled to choose between rights because the interests they protect make incompatible claims. This is as true of the interests protected by a single right as it is of those that are protected by different rights. Often, no action that is open to us can avoid doing injury to some of them. The question may not be which interest is to be harmed. It may be how much harm we do to each.

Choices of this kind are not avoided in liberal theories that claim to eschew any kind of maximization. They arise in any case, when the interests that give content to rights clash with one another. Every right is a bundle of potentially rival claims, because the interests that any right protects are many, and often at odds. Once again, the supposed simplicity of liberal principles is undone by conflicts of value.

Rights are conclusions, not foundations. Claims about rights are the end-products of long and complicated chains of reasoning. When our views of human interests diverge, so do our views of rights. Political philosophies in which rights are claimed to be fundamental pass over these conflicts of value. Yet, because they are endemic in political life, conflicts of value re-emerge in disputes over the rights we possess.

Mill's liberalism has many advantages over rights-based political philosophies. Mill does not begin On Liberty with an appeal to rights. He tells us that the argument in support of his principle of liberty will not appeal to 'the idea of abstract right, as a thing independent of utility'.[17] Instead it is founded on claims about human interests. Even so, Mill's principle founders on the same conflicts that defeat Rawls.

Like many liberal thinkers, Mill sought to frame a principle for the restraint of liberty that could be accepted by all reasonable people. He writes:

> The object of this Essay is to assert one very simple principle, as entitled to govern absolutely the dealings of society with the individual in the way of compulsion and control, whether the means used be physical force in the form of legal penalties, or the moral coercion of public opinion. That principle is, that the sole end for which mankind are warranted, individually or collectively, in interfering with the liberty of action of any of their number, is self-protection.[18]

Mill's 'one very simple principle' is quite different from Rawls's Greatest Equal Liberty Principle. It does not enjoin that liberty be restrained only for the sake of liberty. It tells us that liberty may be restrained only for the sake of preventing harm to others. Whatever its difficulties, this is a useful rule of thumb in any liberal philosophy.

Unlike Rawls's principle, Mill's says nothing about the greatest liberty. Nor does Mill seek to protect any fixed set of basic liberties. True, Mill's principle rules out entirely restraint of liberty in the absence of harm to others; but in doing so it specifies only a necessary condition of justified restraint. It does not tell us which liberties to protect.

Consider policies on the control of dangerous drugs. Mill's principle could mandate the legalization of such drugs in con-

texts, like that of the United States today, where drug use is
pandemic and a policy of prohibition is ineffective and costly.
At the same time, it would not mandate legalization in contexts such as contemporary Japan, in which the use of such
drugs is limited and a policy of prohibition is effective at low
cost. Mill's principle underwrites different regimes for the
control of drug use in different historical and social contexts.
This is true however harm is understood.

Which liberties Mill's principle protects is determined by
applying the principle of utility. By comparison with Rawls's
theory, this may be an advantage. Because he accepts that
different combinations of liberty and restraint will be right
in different circumstances, Mill has no need to circumvent
conflicts among liberties by 'regulating' or 'adjusting' them.
He can face up to the demands of rival freedoms and make
reasonable choices between them. As a result, Mill can read-
ily accept that different combinations of liberties may be desirable in different circumstances. Indeed his principle requires
that there be such varying mixes. In these respects, Mill –
unlike Rawls – has commonsense on his side.

There is a larger difference between Mill's liberalism and
the Rawlsian variety. By contrast with Rawls, Mill does not
suppose that political philosophy aims to design an ideal constitution. Instead he seeks to give guidance to legislators. Mill
does not imagine that a constitution could be designed in which
all important liberties are somehow pre-reconciled. Rather,
he seeks to give legislators guidance as to how conflicts among
them are to be settled.

Mill's principle is not much help in achieving this aim.
Despite what Mill tells us, applying it is no simple matter; but
the difficulties are not those on which most of his critics have
fastened. It is not because there is no sphere of conduct in
which what we do cannot harm others that Mill's principle
fails to do the job he wanted from it. It is because whether
someone has been harmed cannot be determined just by ex-
amining the facts of the matter.

People with divergent conceptions of the good make different judgements about what constitutes harm.[19] Having
different views of human interests, they are bound to make

different judgements about what constitutes a set-back to them. They will therefore give differing accounts of whether people have been harmed in particular cases. Moreover, the harms that Mill's principle requires us to assess cannot always be evaluated in ways that all reasonable people will accept. If we differ as to the content of human well-being, we will differ as to what harms well-being.

To be sure, much disagreement on social and political issues arises from different beliefs regarding the facts of the case. Assessing the long-term effects of different policies is not easy. There are complex chains of cause and effect and difficult counterfactual claims to be evaluated. The difficulties of arriving at an accurate view of society are formidable, and help to account for many of our disagreements on issues such as drug control. Even so, our differing views of the facts of the matter are not the deepest source of our continuing failure to reach consensus in our judgements of harm.

Even where there is agreement on the facts of the matter, people with different views of human well-being will disagree on whether harm has been done. Or, if they agree that harm has been done, they will differ on its severity. Accordingly, if they attempt to apply Mill's principle they will differ as to whether restraint of liberty is justified. Mill's principle does not enable people with different conceptions of the good to reach agreement on whether liberty should be restrained. On the contrary, people with different conceptions of the good will disagree on how Mill's principle is to be applied.

Mill's principle does not enable us to avoid making moral judgements. It requires them. In *Utilitarianism* Mill proposed that different pleasures be ranked by considering which of them is preferred by experienced judges. As we have seen, this account of the higher pleasures founders on the fact that experienced judges prefer different pleasures. Mill's attempt in *On Liberty* to formulate 'one very simple principle' runs aground on a parallel truth: reasonable people disagree in their judgements of harm.

The real problems of Millian liberalism arise in making the utilitarian assessments that the principle of liberty requires.[20] Mill's principle tells us when restraint of liberty *may* be

justified, not when it *is* justified. To know the latter we must
make a utilitarian comparison of the harms and benefits that
result from restraining liberty. Doing so requires an account
of harm which yields the same results when it is used by
people with different conceptions of the good.

If they are to reach the same results when they apply Mill's
principle, people must make the same judgements of the relative importance for human interests of a wide range of harms;
but conflicting judgements on these matters flow from different views of human interests. We cannot apply Mill's principle of liberty without comparing harms; but we will make
different comparative judgements of harm according to
our different views of human interests.

Judgements of the relative importance of different harms
cannot be value-neutral. They pick out different human interests as being weighty. Even where they pick out the same
interests they may rank them differently. Judgements of harm
vary with differing ideals of the good life. That is why Mill's
principle has different results when it is applied by people
whose ideals of the good life are different. Yet again, the seeming simplicity of liberal principles is destroyed by conflicts of
value.

Consensus on the facts cannot of itself yield agreement in
judgements of harm. Rival views of the good will still produce different estimates of the harm that is prevented – and
incurred – by alternative policies. Think again of prohibition
and legalization as alternative ways of controlling harmful
drugs. Agreement on the numbers of addicts that are likely
under each policy and on other salient facts will not yield
agreement on which policy best reduces harm. Judgements of
harm embody our different moral outlooks as much as they
track the facts. For some, addiction is harmful only insofar as
it involves harm to interests. For others, addiction is a harm in
itself, inasmuch as it diminishes personal autonomy.

Where their conceptions of happiness are at odds, classical
utilitarians and liberal utilitarians make different judgements
about harm. James Fitzjames Stephen thought little of personal autonomy as an element of happiness or well-being.
Along with Jeremy Bentham and James Mill, Stephen viewed

negative liberty and security as its most essential ingredients. By contrast, while sharing this view of the importance of negative liberty and security, John Stuart Mill thought personal autonomy – or individuality, as he sometimes referred to it – to be one of the most vitally important human interests. The many differences between Mill and Stephen on issues of restraint of liberty are not accidental. They mirror their different conceptions of human interests. No more than any other can Mill's principle of liberty avoid running aground on conflicts of value.[21]

The failure of Mill's attempt to state a principle of liberty which can be applied without making judgements of value is analogous to that of Karl Popper's account of politics in terms of problem-solving.[22] Popper imagines that there is a consensus on what counts as a problem in society. He fails to perceive that different moral outlooks yield different accounts of social problems. For a traditional religious moralist, homosexuality may be a problem; for a secular liberal it is not. For a liberal, the break-up of families may have bad consequences, but in itself it need not be regrettable; for a traditional moralist, family break-up is inherently bad. For egalitarian liberals, equality is desirable in itself; for other liberals, it is desirable only when inequality is socially damaging.

Contrary to Popper, there is not much consensus on the problems of society, still less on their solutions. Moreover, even where a consensus exists about what counts as a social problem, reasonable people may differ on what would be an acceptable solution. Few solutions are cost-free; many of society's problems are not fully soluble; solving one problem frequently creates others; and so on. What constitutes a reasonable solution to an agreed social problem is as intractably disputed as what counts as a serious harm.

Applying Mill's 'one very simple principle' is, then, an extraordinarily problematic business. No calculus of harms can be constructed that is neutral, or silent, regarding rival views of the good. The judgements of harm that the principle requires are inherently controversial. In many cases, whether Mill's principle has been met will always be a matter of dispute.

The provenance of Mill's principle is a utilitarian concern with well-being, not Kantian ideas of right. Millian liberalism takes for granted that the liberties that best advance human well-being will vary with circumstances. In any comparison with Rawlsian liberalism, these are considerable advantages. Yet the project Mill attempted in *On Liberty* was foredoomed to failure. No single principle can govern the restraint of liberty. All such principles are defeated by conflicts of value.

When we ask which liberties are to be promoted and which restrained, none of the principles advanced by liberal philosophers gives much guidance. Since reasonable people differ in how they resolve conflicts of value, they apply these principles in different and sometimes incompatible ways.

This is not a peculiar difficulty of liberal principles that prioritize liberty. It besets liberal ideals in which other values are given priority. Liberal philosophies in which equality is meant to be the core value are no less undone by it.

We cannot know what it means to treat people as equals unless we know what their interests are. (We do not want to treat people as equals in matters that are of no importance to them.) But different views of interests support rival views of equality, and any sensible view of equality must recognize that interests conflict.

People who cleave to different views of equality will not agree about what it means to treat people as equals. When equalities conflict, such people will resolve their conflicts differently. Contrary to many recent claims,[23] there is no best interpretation of what equality means or requires. Ideals of equality differ, not because they express rival philosophies of right, but because they pick out different human interests as being most important for well-being. In doing so, conflicting principles of equality serve rival conceptions of the good.

Rival egalitarian ideals pick out different goods to be equalized. For some, equality of resources is what justice requires; for others it is equality of welfare; for yet others equality of need-satisfaction. Some theories assert that justice demands equal distribution not of any particular goods but rather of the opportunity to acquire them. Still others claim that equality applies only to rights (while differing on the rights we have).

Promoting equality of the kind that is required by any of these ideals will result in inequalities of the sorts condemned by the rest. None of these rival equalities is more demonstrably fundamental than the others, or more genuinely egalitarian.

Rawls's celebrated difference principle, which claims to capture our sense of fairness better than any rival principle, owes its appeal to the illusion that it reconciles rival equalities. The principle says that that measure of inequality in holdings of primary goods is just which maximizes the holdings of the worst-off in society. Let us set aside the question of how one decides what is a primary good and the difficulty that applying the difference principle requires knowledge of the causes and consequences of different distributions of primary goods that no public authority can reasonably hope to possess. The most fundamental difficulties of Rawls's conception of equality are to be found elsewhere.

Rawls tells us that the primary goods are defined as 'rights, liberties and opportunities, income and wealth, and the social bases of self-respect; these are things that individuals are presumed to want whatever else they want, or whatever their final ends.'[24] Rawlsian equality presupposes that these primary goods are mutually reinforcing or (as it is sometimes put) cross-linked. If, however, the primary goods are often conflicting, and if no choice among rival primary goods is uniquely reasonable, then the difference principle cannot be applied. We are bound to choose which primary goods the worst-off need most.

Greater opportunities may not lead to higher incomes – particularly for those whose incomes are lowest. Better healthcare may enable people to lead longer lives, but better education may boost their self-respect. As we have seen, basic liberties may themselves be rivals. Improving the lot of the worst-off is not a single, unambiguous ideal. It requires difficult choices for which Rawls's principle of equality gives little guidance.

In fact there is no ideal or principle of equality by appeal to which conflicts between equalities can be arbitrated. Divergent views of the good life will give priority to different human interests and thereby to different equalities. Rival views of human interests support rival ideals of equality. Even a single, agreed ideal of equality will be applied differently by people who attach differing weights to its various ingredients.

Like any other ideal, equality is not a simple good. It is a complex combination of competing goods. Equalizing the satisfaction of basic needs will result in an unequal distribution of resources; rewarding merit equally will leave basic needs unequally met; and so on. Rival ideals of equality embody rival views of the good. Each of these conceptions harbours conflicting values.

Within the conceptions of the good that underpin rival ideals of equality, different values are recognized that may conflict and are sometimes incommensurable. A policy that aims to meet basic medical needs equally may have to choose between relieving pain and prolonging life; one that aims to reward educational achievement equally may have to choose between aiding gifted children and helping the disabled. Each of the different components of these rival ideals is itself a site of conflicting values.

There is no best interpretation of equality that can tell us how to resolve these conflicts. Nor can we simply plump for one kind of equality. Whatever we plump for is itself riven by conflict. When equality makes incompatible demands, these conflicts cannot be settled by principles of right, for such principles have a definite content only inasmuch as they express a view of the good.

Conflicts among incommensurable values arise both between and within conceptions of the good. No 'theory of justice' can resolve, or avoid, these conflicts. They can be resolved, if at all, only by reference to the understandings of the good that are found in particular ways of life. Typically, if not invariably, the ideal of the good that animates any way of life will be an amalgam of potentially incompatible ingredients. Normally, it will not favour any one solution over all others, and those who belong to the way of life will be able to argue with equal force for a number of different solutions. Even within a single way of life, such conflicts can be resolved only through a compromise. When a society contains a number of ways of life, a settlement of the claims of rival equalities must involve finding a compromise among several views of the good.

To hold that there are no universal principles for settling conflicts among different ideals of equality does not mean that we must accept the particular understandings of fairness that currently prevail. Indeed, we cannot do so, for they are often unclear or contested. This is a fundamental objection to Hegelian accounts of local justice that have been advanced as alternatives to the universalist interpretations of equality favoured by Kantian liberals.

Michael Walzer has contended that different understandings of what is just or equal apply in different spheres of social life.[25] He notes that what equality means in families is different from what it means in a school or a marketplace. Now it is true that many people believe that different principles of distribution apply in different social contexts. Equally, it is true that their different views of justice in these contexts derive from different understandings of the goods at issue. Insofar as it acknowledges the dependency of principles of right on understandings of the good, Walzer's account marks an advance on that of Rawls.

Nevertheless, his interpretation of equality in terms of spheres of justice breaks down on the fact that there is not enough consensus on the scope and content of these spheres. The sphere of family life is a familiar example. It is viewed in one way by liberals, another by feminists and yet another by traditional moralists and (some) immigrant communities. It is not that there is no shared understanding of the family in contemporary society. Rather, there are several.

In practice, different views of the sphere of the family translate into different judgements about social justice. People who understand the family differently have divergent, sometimes opposed, views of equality. In these circumstances, conflicts about equality cannot be resolved by appealing to a cultural consensus on spheres of justice. When society harbours several ways of life there is too little in the way of such a consensus for that to be possible. Walzer's account gives little guidance about how the conflicting equalities that are demanded today are to be reconciled.

Liberal philosophies in which a principle of equality is central are no less undermined by conflicts of value than those which aim to prioritize liberty. Principles of right with regard to liberty or equality offer no escape from conflicts of value. When conflicts break out within liberal ideals, liberal principles cannot solve them; they break down on such conflicts.

When it is applied to liberty, or any other core liberal value, value-pluralism does not support liberal principles. Rather, liberal principles are subverted by value-pluralism. Core liberal values are sites of conflicts which liberal principles cannot resolve.

Even liberal political philosophies that are based on conflicts of value cannot avoid this fate. In different ways, Isaiah Berlin and Joseph Raz have attempted to found liberal ideals on conflicts of value. By so doing they have given us the best defences of liberal ideals in our time. Yet neither succeeds in giving them an authority that is universal.

Berlin aims to derive the value of liberty from the conflicts of other values. As a value-pluralist, he believes that the goods of life are irreducibly many, that often they cannot be combined, and that in some of the cases where they conflict there is no solution acceptable to all reasonable people. For Berlin, the value of negative liberty is that it enables people to make their own choices among conflicting goods and evils whose value cannot be compared.

Unlike many liberal thinkers, Berlin is fully aware that liberties conflict. He is no less clear that, when they do, comparing different bundles of them so as to identify the one which promotes the greatest freedom takes us little further: 'It may well be', he notes 'that there are many incommensurable kinds and degrees of freedom, and that they cannot be drawn up on any single scale of magnitude.'[26] What Berlin does not note is that, if this is so, then the traditional liberal ideal of the priority of liberty has little meaning.

A libertarian calculus is an impossibility. Whether they be positive or negative, liberties cannot be individuated and then counted. Different conceptions of liberty yield different enumerations of the liberties present in the same situation. For a Benthamite, the liberty of the rapist must be counted as well as that of the rapist's victim. For a Kantian or a Locklan for whom liberty is a strongly normative idea to do with how one is entitled to act, there may be no such thing as the liberty to rape, and therefore no need to count the rapist's liberty.

Even if liberties could be counted, the greatest liberty would not be the largest number of liberties. On any reasonable view, liberties differ greatly in weight. Often we cannot agree on their weights, since we do not agree on the importance of the human interests they advance or protect. As a consequence, even where we agree in counting and ranking our liberties, we may still disagree on the combination of them that best promotes liberty. In that case, even if we agree that liberty must be promoted over other goods, we will disagree about which liberties are to be promoted.[27]

If there are many sorts of liberty whose value cannot be assessed on any single scale, there can be no single structure of negative and positive liberty that is best. Negative and positive liberties are rival goods; one negative liberty from coercion or interference will conflict with another; a positive freedom which protects one aspect of personal autonomy will compete with one that protects a different aspect of autonomy; some facets of autonomy can be promoted only by restraining some negative liberties; and so on. No solution of such conflicts can be uniquely reasonable, or right.

Berlin's derivation of the priority of liberty from conflicts among other values fails. On his own account, conflicts between liberties can be settled only by invoking other values. But there is no impassable barrier that marks off freedom from other values.

It is not that we find out how much freedom there is in a given situation, and then assess its value. Rather, our judgement of how much freedom there is in any given context follows from our values. If this is so, the liberal ideal of giving liberty priority over other goods has no meaning.

Berlin has written truly that 'Each thing is what it is: liberty is liberty, not equality or fairness or justice or culture, or human happiness or a quiet conscience.'[28] Yet, when values clash, what is most at issue is often *which* values are in conflict. 'Justice', 'liberty' and 'welfare' are not territories marked off from one another by impermeable conceptual walls, but sites of conflicting goods, whose boundaries are contested and shifting.

Like Berlin, Joseph Raz grounds the value of liberty in the conflict of values; but the liberty that is so derived is not chiefly freedom from coercion. It is the freedom to be part-author of one's life – the freedom of autonomy (which in many contexts presupposes or encompasses freedom from coercion). The value of autonomy is that it enables us to choose between values where reason cannot arbitrate. Autonomy is valuable because by exercising it each of us can choose among forms of life whose worth cannot be compared. If, according to Berlin, the truth of value-pluralism supports the priority of negative liberty, in Raz's account it is the ideal of autonomy which is mandated by value-pluralism.

Raz does not believe that autonomy is a necessary ingredient in good human lives. He is clear that many flourishing lives lack it:

> I think that there were, and there can be, non-repressive societies, and ones which enable people to spend their lives in worthwhile pursuits, even though their pursuits and the options open to them are not subject to individual choice. Careers may be determined by custom, marriages arranged by parents, child-bearing and child-rearing controlled only by sexual passion and traditions, part-time activities few and traditional, and engagement in them required rather than optional. In such societies, with little mobility, even friends are not chosen. . . . I do not see that the absence of choice diminishes the value of human relations or the display of excellence in technical skills, physical ability, spirit and enterprise, leadership, creativity or imaginativeness, which can all be encompassed in such lives.[29]

The implication of Raz's observation is that among the many varieties of the best human lives there are some in which personal autonomy is lacking. Here he points to a profound truth. Yet in *The Morality of Freedom*, Raz holds that being autonomous is a necessary part of living well in modern societies. He writes that autonomy is an ideal particularly suited to the conditions of the industrial age and its aftermath with their fast changing technologies and free movement of labour. They call for an ability to cope with changing technological, economic and social conditions, for an ability to adjust, to acquire new skills, to move from one subculture to another, to come to terms with new scientific and moral views.[30]

Raz's argument is that unless one can live as an autonomous agent one cannot live well in a modern society. Here the value of autonomy derives from its social and historical context – that of a fast-changing modern society which demands highly developed capacities of choice-making from its members.

This argument has been effectively criticized by Bhikhu Parekh.[31] He notes that some non-western countries, such as Japan and Singapore, have adapted well to technological and economic change, individually and collectively, without apparently accepting personal autonomy as a core value. The same is true of Asian immigrants in western countries: they have done well in the terms of their host societies and in terms of their own well-being *without* adopting personal autonomy as an ideal. These are telling counter-examples to the claim that people cannot flourish in modern conditions unless they live as autonomous agents.

Parekh's criticism can be taken further. Raz's argument takes for granted that immigrant communities whose ways of life do not honour liberal values are bound in time to assimilate to the liberal majority cultures of their host societies. It may be partly because Raz assumes there is no long-term alternative to assimilation that he insists – against the evidence – that adopting liberal values is a necessary condition of flourishing in modern conditions.

The claim that modern conditions require personal autonomy as a condition of individual well-being trades on Enlightenment assumptions regarding the modern world. It presupposes that as societies become more modern so they become more homogeneous in their values. It takes for granted that they will at the same time become more similar to one another. And it presumes that the values upon which they converge are liberal values favouring personal autonomy. None of these assumptions is well founded.

The background idea in Raz's account of autonomy is a society in which the majority accepts its value, but in which there are minorities that do not. The picture presented in *The Morality of Freedom* is that of a predominantly liberal society containing a few non-liberal enclaves, which are bound over time to disappear. Raz's argument is that people will do well only if they assimilate to this liberal, autonomy-valuing majority. His tacit assumption is that as they become modern all or most societies will come to have such a majority.

In fact late modern societies are highly diverse. Sweden, Brazil, France and Poland are modern countries. If they resemble one another, it is in the fact that each of them contains different ways of life. There are few signs that they, or other late modern societies, will converge on a liberal monoculture.

The interaction of liberal with non-liberal ways of life has no outcome that is pre-ordained. In some countries, such as Israel and Turkey, it may have already resulted in a society that contains no majority culture, liberal or otherwise. In many cases, a plural society of this kind is a more likely outcome of the interaction of liberal and non-liberal ways of life than the assimilation of the latter into the former. If history is our guide, there is no enduring connection between becoming modern and valuing personal autonomy.[32]

These considerations suggest a fundamental objection to Raz's argument. A contextual argument to the value of personal autonomy is inherently patchy and exception-ridden. It is bound to fall far short of showing that autonomy is a necessary condition of individual well-being for all or most people in all or even most late modern societies.

In the end, Raz's most basic argument for the value of autonomy seems not to be a contextual or historical one. He writes that 'it would be wrong to identify the ideal [of autonomy] with the ability to cope with the shifting dunes of modern society. Autonomy is an ideal of self-creation. There were autonomous people in many past periods, whether or not they themselves or others around them thought of this as an ideal way of being.'[33] Raz believes that autonomy has value because it enables us to chart our own course among rival values. 'The ideal of personal autonomy is the vision of people controlling, to some degree, their own destiny, fashioning it through successive decisions throughout their lives.'[34] According to Raz, then, what makes autonomy valuable is that it enables individuals to make their own choices among options and lives that are valuable but incompatible:

> Value-pluralism . . . represents the view that there are many different and incompatible valuable ways of life. . . . Value-pluralism is intimately associated with autonomy. . . . Autonomy is valuable only if one steers a course for one's life through significant choices among diverse and valuable options. The underlying idea is that autonomous people had a variety of incompatible opportunities available to them that would have enabled them to develop their lives in different directions. . . .'[35]

Like Berlin's argument for the value of negative liberty, Raz's argument for the value of personal autonomy appeals to value-pluralism. Like Berlin's, it comes unstuck on a consequence of value-pluralism. If value-pluralism is true, personal autonomy cannot be accorded priority over other values.

There are many rival autonomies, and no agreed ways of telling when autonomy on balance has been best advanced. People with different conceptions of human well-being will assess relative autonomy differently. They will specify different states of affairs – options, individual lives or entire societies – as those in which autonomy is best realized. Nor is this just a problem of measurement. It has implications for practice when, as is often the case, some aspects or exercises of personal autonomy are incompatible with others.

Assessments of relative autonomy have all the difficulties that beset judgements about the greatest liberty. They always encompass evaluations of the worth of the life that has been autonomously chosen. People who share an ideal of autonomy may still differ in their estimates of greater and lesser autonomy. When it is pursued by people with differing views of what makes human lives worthwhile, the liberal project of promoting autonomy can have very different outcomes.

Except at the margin, where nearly all capacity for choice has been removed, we have no measure of choice that does not involve making judgements about the good. When we judge that choice is greater in one context than it is in another, we do so on the basis of an evaluation of the options that they contain. We have no value-free measure of relative autonomy. No more than negative liberty can personal autonomy be assessed without invoking an account of the good life.

Autonomy is not free-standing. It is a complex achievement, encompassing (among a good many other necessary ingredients) the absence of coercion, the possession and exercise of skills in choice-making and an environment which contains an array of options that are worth choosing. Judgements of autonomy stand on a view of the good life. They are always grounded in beliefs about what makes life worth living. When the various ingredients of autonomy are given differing degrees of importance, these differences express rival views of the good.

Consider debates arising among people who share a commitment to personal autonomy about how cities are to be planned. Which type of transport system best promotes the personal autonomy of city-dwellers? Which kinds of housing? Recent liberal thought encourages the belief that autonomy is an all-purpose good that can be promoted for everybody without evaluating their disparate projects and purposes; but this is an illusion.

Because they incorporate assessments of the worth of the array of options that autonomous persons can choose from, policies aiming to promote autonomy cannot avoid favouring some options, some purposes, some projects, some values, over others. A city-planner cannot design a transport system without taking a view as to the relative importance of work and leisure in city-dwellers' lives, nor can homes be devised which do not embody some estimate of the worth of families and other relationships whereby people come to cohabit.

There are many reasons why it is difficult to design a widely acceptable policy on public transport aside from the fact that people have different conceptions of the good life. Commonly, different groups have conflicting interests in the funding of such policies. Moreover, their implementation frequently involves making difficult trade-offs among the organized interests of country-dwellers and those who live in towns, the manufacturers of cars and those who supply other kinds of transport, and so on. But these familiar conflicts of group interest are only a part of the difficulties that city-planners face.

The deeper problems come with the conflicting interests of reasonable individuals and the competing claims of different ways of life. Individuals may value a form of city life in which they can shop and work near where they live. At the same time, they may value the low prices and range of goods available in out-of-town shopping malls and the high incomes made possible by long-distance commuting. The cost of small-town living may be high prices and limited choice. The cost of a form of life devoted to high incomes and consumer choice may be a hideous post-urban sprawl. No one trade-off among these conflicting interests is uniquely reasonable.[36]

Equally, city-planners cannot overlook the fact that their decisions can spell life or death for communities. Failing to provide public transport to rural communities can trigger a flight to the cities on the part of new generations. Putting roads through the centres of cities can uproot long-established street communities. There is no escaping these choices. They cannot be made by applying a liberal ideal of personal autonomy. City-planners cannot avoid taking a view on the worth of the ways of life their decisions affect.

The argument is perfectly general, and applies well beyond the sphere of city-planning. Public policies are contested not only because they have different effects on different interests. They support and undermine different ways of living. Disputes about the effects of public policies cannot be settled by appealing to a liberal ideal of personal autonomy. For different conceptions of the good will yield different accounts of the impact of these policies on personal autonomy.

The point is not just that neutrality on such issues is not an option. It is that a liberal commitment to personal autonomy itself compels an evaluation of the worth of different ways of living. Such evaluations necessarily inform our assessments of the relative autonomy of people in different social contexts. If we differ as to the worth of different ways of life, then we will differ in our judgements of relative autonomy.

These differences are relevant to practice, because – like negative liberties – different facets of personal autonomy are often at odds. When different autonomies are rivals, there is often no one solution of their conflict that all are bound to accept, or which none can reasonably reject. Rival autonomies can be incommensurably valuable. When this is so, it is because the goods and ways of life to which they belong are incommensurate in worth.

Autonomy is not a good that can be accorded priority over other values and thereafter promoted. Just as there are incompatible negative liberties, so there are rival autonomies. When autonomy makes conflicting demands, they may reasonably be resolved in different ways. Autonomy cannot be hived off from other values. The line between autonomy and other values is frequently unclear. In many cases goods that seem to be wholly distinct from autonomy shape the options in terms of which autonomy is defined.

It is true that, on any reasonable view, some goods must be distinct from autonomy. Peace; a natural environment in which the interests of future human generations, and of other animal species, are not endangered by human activity; the reduction of disease and poverty – these are goods that do not entail or presuppose the presence of personal autonomy. However it is understood, autonomy cannot be taken to encompass all good things.

Further, some conceptions of the good do not recognize autonomy. In many ways of life, personal autonomy is not valued, or is disvalued. For some fundamentalists, mystics and hedonists, personal autonomy may be irrelevant to the good life, or else a hindrance. That some moralities reject the liberal virtue of personal autonomy is proof that it is distinct from other goods.

Despite this, there are many contexts in which the distinction between autonomy and other goods is reasonably disputed. Think again of cities. Among the goods of city life, freedom to stroll and saunter, to enjoy public spaces in safety and to encounter strangers without fear are – or used to be – centrally important. For one who understands cities as social institutions that encompass these goods, the idea that a city-dweller could be reasonably autonomous and yet lack them is oxymoronic. One who holds to this view of city life may be inclined to say that no city-dweller can be autonomous who lacks the freedoms that go with living well in a city.

In other conceptions of city life, the amenities of living in cities may take second place to the role of cities as sites for the creation of wealth and employment. Cities may be understood as places where we work, while we live – or aspire to live elsewhere. Someone who holds to this latter conception of city life orders the array of options needed to support the autonomy of city-dwellers differently than I do. We differ on what are the right policies for supporting autonomy in cities, as we are likely to do in other areas of social policy, because our views of the human good diverge. As with negative liberty, our judgements of personal autonomy do not stand on their own feet. They express rival views of the good life.

When we differ about what best promotes autonomy, it may be because we understand autonomy differently. Or it may be because, though we share a common understanding of autonomy, we differ on how autonomy is to be traded off against other goods which we also recognize. In either case, what accounts for our differences may be that we have made different judgements in conflicts among incommensurable values.

Like Berlin's, Raz's attempt to ground liberal ideals in value-pluralism founders on conflicts of value. We cannot agree on what most advances autonomy, because our views of the good diverge in precisely the ways of which value-pluralism speaks. No more than harm to others or negative liberty can an ideal of autonomy stand aloof from contending conceptions of the good. Autonomy is not a still point in the turning world of rival values. It is a point of intersection for all their conflicts.

However they are defined, liberal principles do not offer the refuge from conflict that recent orthodoxies in political philosophy have promised. Neither libertarian nor egalitarian

principles can resolve conflicts among liberal values. The belief that they enable us to do so is the opposite of the truth.
They break down into indeterminacy or arbitrariness whenever they face these conflicts.

It does not matter whether liberal values are conceived in
terms of the promotion of autonomy, the priority of negative
liberty, the demands of equality, the protection of human
rights or – though this is the most useful rule of thumb that
liberal philosophy has produced – the prevention of harm to
others. In every case, liberal values prescribe rival freedoms.
By so doing they engender dilemmas for which liberal principles have no answer.

If we think of liberalism as a prescription for an ideal regime, it is undone by conflicts of value that liberal principles
are powerless to resolve. It is better to step back from Kant to
Hobbes, and think of the liberal project as the pursuit of *modus
vivendi* among conflicting values.

4

Modus Vivendi

Liberalism contains two philosophies. In one, toleration is justified as a means to truth. In this view, toleration is an instrument of rational consensus, and a diversity of ways of life is endured in the faith that it is destined to disappear. In the other, toleration is valued as a condition of peace, and divergent ways of living are welcomed as marks of diversity in the good life. The first conception supports an ideal of ultimate convergence on values, the latter an ideal of *modus vivendi*. Liberalism's future lies in turning its face away from the ideal of rational consensus and looking instead to *modus vivendi*.

The predominant liberal view of toleration sees it as a means to a universal civilization. If we give up this view, and welcome a world that contains many ways of life and regimes, we will have to think afresh about human rights and democratic government. We will refashion these inheritances to serve a different liberal philosophy.

We will come to think of human rights as convenient articles of peace, whereby individuals and communities with conflicting values and interests may consent to coexist. We will think of democratic government not as an expression of a universal right to national self-determination, but as an expedient, enabling disparate communities to reach common decisions and to remove governments without violence. We will think of these inheritances not as embodying universal principles, but as conventions, which can and should be refashioned in a world of plural societies and patchwork states.

The aim of human rights is not to project a single regime, political or economic, throughout the world. It is to assure *modus vivendi* among regimes that will always be different. There are some rights that all regimes must meet if they are to be reasonably legitimate in contemporary conditions; but the rights that such regimes protect are not all the same. A regime in which all rights are fully protected is not even imaginable. However they are conceived, human rights make conflicting demands, whose conflicts can be rightly reconciled in different ways.

Human rights are not immutable truths, free-standing moral absolutes whose contents are self-evident. They are conventions, whose contents vary as circumstances and human interests vary. They should be regarded not as a charter for a worldwide regime, liberal or otherwise, but rather as embodying minimum standards of political legitimacy, to be applied to all regimes.

Manifestly, not all actually existing regimes are equally legitimate. Just as some ways of life do better than others in resolving universal conflicts, so do some regimes. A regime that resolves a conflict of liberties by moderating them is better than one in which some liberties are extinguished but those that remain are no better protected. Where it can be established, the former regime is (in that respect) more legitimate than the latter. Even so, it is a mistake to think that as regimes become more legitimate they become more alike.

It is profitless to look for criteria for the legitimacy of political regimes that apply in all historical contexts. Some goods and evils are generically human; but the circumstances of human history are too complex and shifting to allow universal values to be translated into a universal theory of political legitimacy. As David Hume understood, the legitimacy of any regime is always partly a matter of historical accident. Monarchies, empires and liberal republics can be no less legitimate in different historical contexts.[1] To this extent, political philosophy is unavoidably time-bound.

In contemporary circumstances, all reasonably legitimate

regimes require a rule of law and the capacity to maintain peace, effective representative institutions, and a government that is removable by its citizens without recourse to violence. In addition, they require the capacity to assure the satisfaction of basic needs to all and to protect minorities from disadvantage. Last, though by no means least, they need to reflect the ways of life and common identities of their citizens.

These requirements are rarely met in full and they are not meant to be exhaustive. It is impossible to specify necessary and sufficient conditions of legitimacy which apply in all circumstances, even those of the late modern world. In the terms set by contemporary liberal orthodoxy, no actually existing regime can be fully legitimate. Indeed, since the demands of rights cannot all be fully honoured even in principle, no conceivable regime is fully legitimate. This is perhaps a *reductio ad absurdum* of rights-based liberalism.

The requirements of legitimacy that all contemporary regimes should meet are not the free-standing rights of recent liberal orthodoxy. They are enforceable conventions, framed to give protection against injuries to human interests that make any kind of worthwhile life impossible. A regime is illegitimate to the extent that its survival depends upon systematic injury to a wide range of these interests.

Regimes in which genocide is practised, or torture institutionalized, that depend for their continuing existence on the suppression of minorities, or of the majority, which humiliate their citizens or those who coexist with them in society, which destroy the common environment, which sanction religious persecution, which fail to meet basic human needs in circumstances where that is practically feasible or which render impossible the search for peace among different ways of life – such regimes are obstacles to the well-being of those whom they govern. Because their power depends on the infliction of the worst universal evils, they are illegitimate, however long-lived they may be.

Such regimes come in many varieties. In some, such as South Africa under the apartheid regime, the majority was denied freedoms and powers assured to a privileged minority. The apartheid system rested on injuries to the vital interests of most of those who were subject to it. It depended on far-reaching restrictions on personal choice and wide inequalities of resources between ethnic groups. The racial groupings that were created with the imposition of apartheid did not reflect the complex and mixed communities that the country had long contained. Above all, the inequality of power on which the system stood prevented the recurrent renegotiation of interests and values that is necessary for any sustainable *modus vivendi*.

In other cases, all are denied vital freedoms, even the most privileged beneficiaries of the regime. In the Stalin regime no-one enjoyed the protection of the access to justice that was available to a small minority in pre-democratic South Africa. The same was true in the Hitler and Mao regimes. Though they all embodied huge disparities of power, these regimes did not rest on inequalities of rights, since none of them contained the institution of the rule of law.

Illegitimate regimes maintain themselves in power in widely different ways. In some, lethal violence is one of the chief instruments of repression. This was true of the Suharto regime in Indonesia, the Duvalier regime in Haiti and the Pinochet regime in Chile. Others are sustained largely by economic sanctions on dissent. In Czechoslovakia during much of the communist period, personal freedom was comprehensively repressed, but lethal violence rare. After the suppression of the 1956 popular rising much the same was true in Hungary. Illegitimate regimes come in many shapes and sizes. They are as diverse as the injuries that can be done to human interests.

Legitimacy is not something that can always be easily decided. An authoritarian regime such as that ruling post-Mao China may protect some of the vital interests of the majority; but insofar as it is engaged in genocidal repression in Tibet its legitimacy becomes questionable. Equally, a liberal democratic regime may be illegitimate insofar as it is too weak or too corrupt to protect the vital interests of the majority, or of minorities. In its last phase, the Yeltsin regime in Russia may have become illegitimate in this way. (That does not mean that its successor will be more legitimate. It could well be worse.) There is no simple test of legitimacy.

Liberal universalists claim that what they take to be liberal values are authoritative for every regime. Liberal relativists deny that there are any universal values. Both are mistaken. There are minimal standards of decency and legitimacy that apply to all contemporary regimes, but they are not liberal values writ large.[2]

If we consider contemporary history we find that regimes which meet these standards are not of one kind. By no means all honour liberal values. Some non-liberal regimes satisfy some standards of legitimacy better than some liberal states.

It would be far-fetched to think of the Ottoman Empire as a liberal regime. Its distinctive institution was the system of *millets* – religious communities that were recognized and protected by law, and which were granted jurisdiction over their own members. The *millet* system did not accord equality of status to non-Muslims or confer protection on non-monotheistic religions. Because it did not provide recognized rights of exit for individuals who wished to leave the communities of their birth, it failed to respect personal autonomy.

Though it disregarded some core liberal values, the Ottoman Empire was a regime of toleration. The system of *millets* protected a diversity of religions. Within a common framework, it enabled their practitioners to live under the legal jurisdiction of their own religious community. At its best, it was a system in which neither common identities nor ultimate loyalties were framed in ethnic terms.[3]

A similar claim may be made on behalf of the Habsburg Empire. It contained few entrenched rights and it recognized no principle of democracy that required national self-determination. Nonetheless, it met minimum standards of legitimacy to do with religious freedom and the treatment of minorities better than some of the avowedly democratic regimes that replaced it.

More recent times afford other examples. The Castro regime in Cuba does not protect liberal freedoms of inquiry or expression. Many vital personal liberties are repressed. At the same time, it has a better record of protecting the interests of its worst-off members than some advanced countries. Over several decades, and until quite recently, Cuba's schools and medical system delivered better education and health-care to the poorest than that received by many disadvantaged Americans. In this example, the value of personal freedom collides with concern for the well-being of the worst-off.

Recent doctrines of human rights embody a confusion between the universal requirements of political legitimacy and the particular claims of liberal values. Though they normally overlap, they are not the same. Highly dissimilar regimes can be equally legitimate. Highly legitimate regimes can be very different.

A regime can be highly legitimate without honouring values that are distinctively liberal. Equally, regimes that are clearly liberal may differ deeply in how they resolve conflicts among rights. There are some human rights that any moderately legitimate regime must recognize and enforce, but they do not add up to an ideal regime, liberal or otherwise. The proper role of human rights is to protect human beings against universal evils.

Not all universal evils can be removed by establishing rights. Some depend on highly complex social conditions and cultural attitudes. Humiliation is a universal evil. Yet no society can prevent humiliation by instituting a right against it. Even if it were possible to frame such a right, many of the innumerable ways in which humans humiliate one another are too subtle to be caught by it.

A society can respect human rights and nevertheless contain practices that inflict the universal evil of humiliation. A society in which human rights are well protected may still have a long way to go before it can consider itself decent. The demands of universal rights are not the same as those of human decency.[4] Above all, the demands of human rights are not the same as those of liberal values (assuming the latter can be stated unambiguously). To think that universal rights require the projection of liberal values throughout the world is to press human rights into the service of a species of liberal fundamentalism.

The Universal Declaration of Human Rights was adopted and promulgated by the General Assembly of the United Nations on 10 December 1948. The rights that are specified for protection in the Declaration reflect the historical events that preceded the founding of the UN. They are a mixture of provisions, some of which deserve to be regarded as marking boundaries of legitimacy in any future we can envisage, while others express political ideals that are much more time-bound. The most weighty of the rights protected in the Declaration prohibit states from engaging in policies of genocide and racial enslavement of the kind which produced the Holocaust. Articles 4 and 5 of the Declaration prohibit slavery and torture. They protect interests that are generically human, injury to which is an obstacle to any kind of worthwhile human life. No regime can reasonably claim legitimacy in which many such interests are systematically violated.

Some of the rights specified in the Declaration are clearly indefensible as universal requirements. Article 24 confers a universal right to periodic holidays with pay. The reason that this cannot plausibly be viewed as a universal right is not that it is a welfare right whose protection requires a positive input of resources. That is true of all human rights: without human and technological resources, including those that confer effective military power, no human right can be safely exercised. Nor is it the fact that there is some indeterminacy in its content. All rights contain significant indeterminacies. Contrary to many doctrinaire accounts, in these respects positive welfare rights stand on all fours with negative passive rights.[5]

The reason Article 24 does not confer a universal right is that it is a provision which makes no sense in communities in which wage-labour is not the dominant institution in working life. It is a specific social or economic ideal, desirable in some contexts, undesirable or irrelevant in others. Though it specifies conditions that particular regimes may have reason to entrench as a right, it cannot sensibly be treated as stating a universal imperative.

Even where Articles of the Declaration confer rights that are defensible as universal requirements, they do not confer a single entitlement. Every right is a bundle of entitlements, each made up of a diversity of claims. Just as one right may conflict with another, so may the demands of a single right collide with each other.

Consider the right to freedom of religion. Article 18 of the Universal Declaration of Human Rights states: 'Everyone has the right to freedom of thought, conscience and religion; this right includes freedom to change his religion or belief, and freedom, either alone or in community with others and in public or in private, to manifest his religion or belief in teaching, practice, worship and observance.'[6]

Among the rights encompassed in freedom of religion are some that frequently collide in practice. In societies with a history of religious conflict and a weak regime of toleration the right to proselytize may work to undermine the right to practise one's religion without fear of persecution. So may other public expressions of religious allegiance.

The right to freedom of religion is a highly complicated jumble of claims protecting human interests that are often at odds. Where the rights that make up freedom of religion collide with one another, their conflicts may rightly be settled in different ways. In Singapore there is full freedom of religious practice and belief, but proselytism is forbidden. In prohibiting missionary activity Singapore does not protect what in liberal societies is regarded as the unfettered exercise of the right to religious freedom. Yet, perhaps partly for that reason, Singapore has in recent times avoided religious strife better than have some liberal regimes.

The Singaporean interpretation of freedom of religion accords with that of some of its early modern advocates. In his *Theologico-Political Treatise*, Benedict de Spinoza wrote: '. . . the rites of religion and the outward observances of piety should be in accordance with public peace and wellbeing, and should therefore be determined by the sovereign power.'[7] Here Spinoza states a caveat which applies to all doctrines of toleration.

However it is understood, toleration is not worth much if it cannot be enforced. It is vain to protect the freedom to proselytize if its consequence is a war of religion in which the state loses the power to protect the freedom to practise one's religion. Any regime of toleration depends for its existence on an authority that can enforce it. The freedoms of public observance and of proselytism must yield (as Spinoza recognized) to the demands of public peace, without which no exercise of freedom of religion can be safe. Like any other right, freedom of religion is not a harmonious set of interlocking freedoms, but a point of intersection for competing claims. Human rights do not dovetail into a harmonious scheme. They protect human interests that are often in conflict. Even the most minimal rights can be rivals. A liberal democracy which resorted to the torture of combatants in a war of survival against a genocidal regime would do wrong. Yet it could still be justified in what it did. The right action may well contain wrong.

Rights are stitched together from a number of strands, each woven from different threads. Under the pressures of circumstance, strands are unpicked and the patchwork unravels. One test of the legitimacy of a regime is its skill in resewing the patchwork of rights.

Recognizing that rights can conflict with one another and that each of them can make conflicting demands does not give us a criterion that can be used to pick out rights that are universal. We do not assert that a right is possessed by all human beings because of any formal properties it may possess, such as consistency with other rights. What supports such a claim is the importance of the human interests which the right protects.

It is no part of the present inquiry to advance any overall theory of rights. If what I have argued is sound, there cannot be a theory of rights – at least of the sort recent liberal thought has tried to develop. The human interests that rights protect are too various and too conflicting for any such theory to be a possibility.

There can be no definitive list of human rights. Rights are not theorems that fall out of theories of law or ethics. They are judgements about human interests whose content shifts over time as threats to human interests change. When we ask which rights are universal, we are not inquiring after a truth that exists already. We are asking a question that demands a practical decision: Which human interests warrant universal protection?

Universal rights offer protection against universal human

evils. There can be no once-for-all list of such rights, since the content of these evils alters with changes in human life. That is why it makes sense to revise or phase out some rights, and to create new rights.[8]

Human interests change, as forms of life change. Before the early modern period in Europe, privacy may not have been a central need in people's lives. Where privacy is not valued it makes no sense to demand it as a right. Where privacy has become a part of a worthwhile life, as perhaps it has in most late modern societies, it deserves to be entrenched as a right.

It is not only changes in what people value that can warrant the establishment of new rights. So can changes in circumstance. The increase of human powers can itself endanger human interests in ways that justify the invention of new rights. New technologies of genetic engineering threaten human interests in novel ways. On the other hand, new circumstances may warrant the curtailment or abolition of established rights. The growth in human population may defeat the claims of any right of procreation. And so on.[9]

As human interests change, so do rights. There is nothing wrong in this. Rights must vary in this way if they are to have any content. We cannot know what content rights have if we do not know which interests they protect. A truly rights-based liberalism, if it could be formulated, would be vacuous.

A universal human right is warranted whenever there is a human interest that ought to be universally protected. Universal human rights can be respected in a variety of regimes. Equally, they can be violated in many regimes, including those which honour liberal values.

Despite being a non-liberal regime, the Ottoman Empire met one of the key requirements of universal rights by enforcing religious toleration. On the other hand, the genocidal massacre by British colonists of the indigenous inhabitants of Van Diemen's Land (present-day Tasmania) violated universal human rights atrociously, though in other contexts they may have honoured liberal values.

This is not to say that universal rights are compatible with any and every way of life. Self-evidently they are not. But they can be honoured and enforced by both liberal and non-liberal regimes. Understood in this way, universal human rights are not an obstacle to *modus vivendi* between different regimes but a condition of it.

Enforcing universal rights may mean overriding a sovereign state. Such action is fraught with hazards. Yet it is sometimes justified. A ground for such interventions exists in the trials held at Nuremberg in the aftermath of the Second World War. Since then there have been other international agreements defining human rights and limiting the authority of sovereign states to infringe them. The United Nations Convention Against Torture which was passed by the General Assembly in 1984 explicitly restricts state sovereignty, 'placing an obligation on states to arrest [torturers] and extradite them, and even to try non-nationals for the offence where extradition is impossible'.[10] The Westphalian conventions that made state sovereignty a central principle in international law in early modern times have long been qualified.

Such legal precedents state a necessary, not a sufficient, condition of the justified enforcement of rights across boundaries and regimes. The sufficient conditions are prudential and moral, not legal. Stated shortly and roughly, they are that the human interests which the rights protect are weighty enough to warrant such intervention – and that the intervention stands a reasonable chance of success. Whether these sufficient conditions are met in any particular case is not something that can be deduced from any theory of rights. It is a matter of judgement.

A worldwide regime of rights is a legitimate project. True, the institutions of global governance that are needed to enforce such a regime are almost infinitely remote from political realities. A world of nearly two hundred sovereign states, many of them deeply corroded or collapsed, others with the capacity to resist any attempt to curb systematic violations of rights in which they are engaged, is not an hospitable environment for the construction of a regime of rights. Moreover, any renewal of military conflict between the world's major powers would make such a regime impractical. Even so, there is nothing inherently unrealizable in the ideal of an international system in which states are held accountable for rights abuses.

Establishing and upholding such a regime, however, entangles us in intractable moral and political conflicts. Where enforcing rights means waging war, or puts other rights at risk, protecting rights may entail violating rights. The barest minimum of rights can engender tragic choices. The best of policies may do wrong. It is a cardinal error to look to any regime of rights to deliver us from these realities.

The tendency of recent liberal political philosophy has been to do precisely that. Contemporary liberal orthodoxy is a species of legalism, in which virtually every important issue of public policy is treated as a question of fundamental rights. The adversarial practice of rights has obscured the permanent necessity of political negotiation and compromise. Rights-based liberalism presents itself as a basis of public justification to which all can assent, regardless of their particular conceptions of the good. In practice, the effect of rights-based liberalism has been to render hard cases in public policy insoluble.

Just as there is no one resolution of conflicts among liberties that is everywhere right, so there is no procedure for resolving such conflicts that is everywhere desirable. Many regimes provide judicial procedures for settling such conflicts. In others, much is left to political decision. Each procedure can be defended in the context of particular traditions and historical circumstances. Yet there are good reasons to resist the trend promoted by recent liberal thought, which has been to inflate the role of rights and hollow out the practice of politics.

Fundamental rights – at least as they are understood in the dominant school of recent liberal thought – are unconditional and overriding. As a result, the upshot of any procedure for adjudicating fundamental rights is bound to be victory for one side and defeat for the other. When this procedure is applied to issues involving conflicts about which society is deeply divided, the result can only be to render them intractable.

Because it has been decided in this way, abortion has become in the United States an issue on which compromise is impossible. The result has been chronic low-intensity civil strife, in which violations of fundamental rights – including the right to life of doctors who perform abortions – are endemic. By treating it as an issue of fundamental rights, an issue which would in any case have been difficult in the context of the United States has been rendered insoluble. In practically every other liberal democracy, access to abortion has been governed by legislation, revisable over time with shifts in social values and circumstances, and embodying a compromise between opposed moral outlooks. In most countries, the settlement that has been reached on abortion is one that accords priority to the interests and choices of women. There is a lesson here for liberal thought. When society contains sharply divergent ethical beliefs, an appeal to basic rights will not produce a settlement that is accepted as legitimate. If we seek a settlement of divisive issues that is legitimate and stable, we have no alternative to the long haul of politics.

From the standpoint of liberal legalism, the shabby compromises that are reached by political negotiation lack the principled legitimacy which is thought to accompany the adjudication of rights. In this contemporary orthodoxy, politics is too veined with the transient, the arbitrary and the morally suspect for its slippery settlements ever to be more than a poor second-best to the majestic certainties of law.

Legalism of this kind is a dangerous turn in liberal thought, and not only because it nurtures delusive hopes of law. Liberal legalism cherishes the illusion that we can dispense with politics. In truth the features of political life that liberal legalists find most suspect are those we can least do without.

Unlike the legal adjudication of universal rights, political settlements are local, variable and renegotiable. So long as democratic institutions are working fairly well, political settlements reached about deeply divisive issues are usually perceived to be more legitimate than legal procedures which end in the promulgation of unconditional rights. Whereas the adjudication of rights is – or at least imagines itself to be – unconditional and final, a political settlement can strike a balance among contending ideals and interests. Nor is that balance fixed for ever. It can shift, as interests and circumstances change, and knowledge of the results of different policies improves. Whereas the adjudication of rights aims for uniformity and finality, the practice of politics allows for changing solutions in different circumstances.

What may be a reasonable policy in some circumstances may be indefensible in others. Wholesale legalization may be a reasonable policy on drug use where, as in the United States and post-communist Russia, it is pandemic. In Norway or Japan such a policy is very likely indefensible. Similarly, American multiculturalism is only one way of organizing a society that contains several ethnic identities and ways of life – and not self-evidently the most successful.

No policy is uniquely reasonable, or even acceptable by all reasonable people. The human interests that are affected cannot all be fully protected. That is why they are often best left to political deliberation. Treating highly contested issues as matters of fundamental rights has not removed them from political contention. It has merely further politicized the practice of law.

Rights-based liberalism is a poor guide for societies riven by opposed ethical beliefs. But communitarian philosophy gives no better guidance. Like the standard varieties of liberal thought, it has not understood that when society harbours a diversity of ways of life, an overarching consensus on values is impossible – as well as undesirable.

Communitarian thinkers have made several forceful criticisms of liberalism.[11] They have pointed out that the autonomous individual of liberal philosophy is a cipher, without a history or any particular identity. Unfortunately, the same is true of the communitarian conception of community.

The recent liberal view of the human subject is a view from nowhere. What liberal thought has theorized is not the human experience of justice and injustice but the intuitions of liberal philosophers. By pointing to the unreality of this liberal view, communitarian thinkers have done political thought a valuable service.

At the same time, the idea of community which communitarian thinkers have deployed is just as far removed from any human reality. It is not one that has ever been known among men and women. It too is a view from nowhere.

The community that haunts communitarian thinking is a

noumenal community, as remote from common experience as the Kantian transcendental subject. Unmoved by the accidents of language, territory or religious allegiance, it lacks the particular histories that define actually existing communities. Like the individual subject in liberal theories of justice, the ideal community of communitarian theory is unmoved by conflicts of interest or value.[12]

In common with the liberal thinkers they attack, communitarian thinkers have a conception of the human subject from which conflict has been erased. That has always been a mistaken view of human life. In present circumstances, it involves repressing the fact that hybridity – the condition whereby individuals belong not to one but to several ways of life, with all their conflicts – has come to shape the identities of many people.

The access to different ways of life that comes with mass immigration and new technologies of communication has made the capacity to harbour dissonant values and views of the world an essential part of many people's lives. A world in which people are defined by membership of a single community is not only far removed from that in which we live. It is not seriously imaginable by us. The unreality of such a world makes any ideal of seamless community dangerous.

In their defence of common life, communitarian thinkers hark back to critics of the Enlightenment such as Herder. Like the Romantics who followed him, Herder argued forcefully that progress towards a universal civilization was not without loss. Against the Enlightenment notion of universal humanity, he contended that what is most essential in the identities of humans is what is most accidental about them. For Herder, it is not what humans have in common that makes them what they are. It is their differences.

According to Herder, the project of a universal civilization is bound to sweep away the different cultures that the species has exfoliated during its history and prehistory, and replace them with an empty abstraction. A civilization founded on this abstraction would not embody universal humanity. It would embody one narrow way of life.

Herder showed that a state cannot be legitimate unless it

reflects the particular histories and identities of its citizens. Yet for us there can be few more perilous illusions than that which is embodied in Herder's Romantic dream of a world of harmonious, organic communities, flowering in peace side by side.

Some of the worst injuries to human well-being in the twentieth century were committed not by universalist regimes but by governments committed to ideals of organic community. If the Nazis had any coherent intellectual outlook, its genealogy was not in any kind of universalism. It was in the Counter-Enlightenment, with its rejection of any common human nature and its appeal to the uniqueness and singular histories of peoples.[13]

But the Counter-Enlightenment belief that there is no such thing as human nature is as much an illusion as the Enlightenment idea of universal humanity. Like other animals, humans have a common nature that is fairly constant in its needs. It is this common nature that underlies universal goods and evils. It is also what accounts for their universal conflicts.

The post-Romantic denial of a common human nature is intelligible only as a species of idealism. It makes sense only if human beings are essentially constituted by their beliefs about themselves. If that were true, all that would be required to bring conflict to an end would be a change in our beliefs. But the causes of moral and political conflict are not finally in our opinions. They are in our needs. It is because the needs of humans are discordant, not because their moral opinions are at odds, that conflicts of value are universal.

Twentieth-century Counter-Enlightenment movements had more in common with the Enlightenment than they knew. They were committed to a denial of conflict among values as far-reaching as that of the most radical Enlightenment universalists. Even their belief that the Enlightenment can be rolled back by an act of will is of a piece with the illusions of Enlightenment humanism. If we shed these illusions, we will understand that the Enlightenment is an historical fate.[14]

In the same way, the coexistence and interpenetration of different ways of life is an unalterable fact. Communities are not now, if they ever were, sealed off from one another. Nor are they any less ridden by conflicts. Even less than at any time in the past are human identities shaped by the values of a single way of life. On the contrary, they are shaped by conflicts between and within communities. Very rarely can individuals choose the identity in terms of which they are perceived by others.

Today, as throughout human history, human identities are primarily ascriptive, not elective. For nearly everyone, belonging to a community is a matter of fate, not choice. A little thought on the history of the twentieth century should be enough to remind us that the ascription of community membership may be a matter of life and death. Any political ideal that neglects these realities can only be pernicious in its consequences.

That communities define themselves and are defined by others in terms of conflicts for control of power and territory; that, in all the actually existing varieties of communities with which we are familiar, they display continuing internal conflicts and struggles; that in strong communities, membership and identity are matters not of choice or self-consciousness but of fate and social recognition; that in the real world of history the shadows cast by communities are hierarchy, subordination and exclusion and, in the worst cases, civil division and war – these long-familiar facts are largely absent from communitarian philosophy. As a result, the communitarian critique of liberalism has brought us no nearer to the conflicts of interests and values that are the proper subject matter of political thought.

What late modern plural societies need is not the consensus on values that communitarians imagine they find in past communities. It is common institutions within which conflicts of interests and values can be negotiated. For us, having a life in common cannot mean living in a society unified by common values. It means having common institutions through which the conflicts of rival values can be mediated.

Common institutions come in many varieties. This is not because there ought to be as many regimes as there are distinctive communities – as some communitarian theorists seem to think. It is because the conditions of coexistence among communities vary too much for one type of regime to be most desirable everywhere.

Communitarian thinkers are right that political legitimacy cannot rest, solely or even chiefly, on abstract principles of justice or rights. If they are to be accepted as legitimate by their citizens, states must give recognition to the common identities of their citizens. But like Herder, communitarian thinkers are mistaken in their belief that political legitimacy depends on the state's mirroring the values of any one community or way of life.

The ideal of a mode of government that mirrors the values of a single community is dangerous because it implies that plural identities are pathological and univocal identities normal. It suggests that intractable conflicts of value are products of error or ill-will, so that nothing other than folly and corruption stands in the way of a world of harmonious communities. This is only Rousseau's dangerous fantasy, anachronistically reinvented by thinkers who have learnt nothing from the history of the twentieth century.

In any future that we can realistically envision, states will be legitimate only if they reflect the plurality and hybridity of common identities. The difficulty comes in meeting this condition. Communitarian thought has little to say on this crucial question. Indeed, in its stress on homogeneity of values in society, it has detached political thought from serious engagement with the needs of the times.

Useful as communitarian philosophy has been as a corrective of the excesses of liberal individualism, the issue that should shape the agenda of political thought is not how to restore strong communities. It is how the diversity of individuals and communities in late modern societies can coexist in common institutions which they accept as legitimate.

Rather than looking to an ideal community to deliver us from conflicts of interests and values, we should view political institutions as expedients whereby these conflicts can be contained. Looking at political institutions in this way enables us to identify respects in which the liberal tradition needs revision.

From Benjamin Constant and John Stuart Mill to John

Rawls, the sovereign nation-state is the great unexamined assumption of liberal thought. It is true that some liberals have rejected the nation-state, and argued for varieties of federalism. But they have been in a minority, and their criticism of the nation-state was vitiated by their mistaken belief that political allegiance could rest on loyalty to principles alone.[15]

Even where liberal thinkers have not explicitly defended the sovereign nation-state, it is presupposed by much of what they argue for. The institution of the nation-state is tacitly assumed by liberal ideals of citizenship. It underpins the assumption of an overlapping consensus on liberal values, and it is presupposed by the notion of social justice as an ideal pattern of distribution. If we wish to renew the liberal project we will need to look beyond the nation-state in many parts of the world.

For the past two hundred years the liberal project has been pursued in most countries through an enterprise of nation-building. Nineteenth-century classical liberals used the powers of the modern state to weaken or destroy local communities and regional loyalties. By doing so they helped to create the autonomous individual. As late modern societies have become more plural, neither the cohesive national cultures nor the autonomous individuals they made possible can any longer be taken as given.

Being an autonomous agent is not, as Kant and his latter-day disciples seem to suppose, the timeless quintessence of humanity. It is a particular way of being human, and for that reason it has a history. Nothing in that history ensures that the autonomous individual has a future. Autonomous individuals are artefacts, made possible by the power of the modern state.

Autonomous individuals came into the world as products of the national cultures created by modern European nation-states. Modern European states did not inherit cohesive national cultures. Using their powers of military conscription, taxation and schooling, they constructed them. By constructing nations, modern states made possible the autonomous individuals of liberal thought and practice.

At their best, the national cultures that underpinned the

classical European nation-state were not communities of blood
and soil, but almost the reverse. Though their origins were
often ethnic, they sometimes achieved a partial transcendence of ethnic identities and allegiances.[16]

In their ideal form, the national cultures constructed by
modern sovereign states harboured a single way of life – that
of autonomous individuals. As the homogeneous national cultures of the past have begun to dissolve, so the way of life of
autonomous individuals is ceasing to be the predominant way
of life in late modern societies. It is only one among many.

Of course the enterprise of constructing an homogeneous
national culture was nowhere completed. All modern European states contain ethnic conflicts and national minorities.
Even France, which is in some ways a paradigm of civic nationhood, has always harboured ethnic nationalist political
movements. At the same time, as in other European countries, the French state is finding it difficult to resist the claims
for recognition of minority cultures. In 1999 a proposal to
support the teaching of minority languages in French schools
had become a political and constitutional issue.[17]

Moreover, by no means all modern European states have
harboured a single national culture. In what sense has there
ever been a Spanish nation – or, for that matter, a British
nation? Neither the Spanish nor the British states are nation-
states. Both are artefacts of monarchy. Still, most West European modern states could once claim to be states in which the
majority of people thought of themselves as belonging in a
single nation. In varying degrees, that is no longer so. Where
plural societies have developed peacefully, increasing numbers of people identify themselves less and less with any single nation-state.

As a result of the development of transnational institutions
in the European Union, national and regional identities are no
longer automatically mutually exclusive. That is one reason
why European nationalist movements are less committed to
achieving independence. A Scot can be a Gael, and at the
same time British and European; a Catalan might conceivably
think of herself as being not only European but also a Spanish
citizen. In parts of Europe, such plural identities are common.

Partly this is a result of a metamorphosis in the nature of war. Since the advent of nuclear weapons, large-scale wars among states of the kind classically theorized by Clausewitz have diminished in number and importance. In their aftermath, varieties of civil war have flourished. Where the prospect of war among states dwindled almost to vanishing-point, as it has done in Western Europe since the Second World War, nation-states have lost some of their primacy as expressions of collective identity. As Clausewitzian war among states has declined, so has the nation-state as the primary object of political allegiance.[18]

Other developments have reinforced this trend. With mass migration and large-scale mobility of labour, the more uniform national cultures of the past are fragmenting into mosaics. At the same time, transnational institutions such as the European Union have co-opted some of the powers that used to be exercised by sovereign states. Both in terms of the societies they govern and the global environment in which they must function, sovereign nation-states have a sharply diminished role.

As a consequence of the emergence of plural identities and the increasing role of transnational institutions, our time may soon resemble the late medieval world more than the early modern era. In a range of contexts, the sovereign nation-state has ceased to be the predominant political institution. It is some time since we ceased living in a Westphalian system of states.

Yet it would be hyperbolic to claim that nation-states are withering away. Nation-states remain the only large-scale institutions of democratic participation. No transnational institution has the democratic legitimacy possessed by some nation-states. In consequence, though nation-states have become weaker, transnational institutions have not at the same time grown stronger.

Again, alongside the decline of the classical European nation-state there has been an ominous growth of ethnic nationalism. If, in most of Western Europe, classical nation-states allowed for a partial transcendence of ethnic identities and allegiances, in Eastern Europe and the Balkans this European model had the opposite result. There European ideals of nationality have proved an inspiration for ethnic nationalism. As homogeneous national cultures have waned in Western Europe's long postwar peace, waxing ethnic nationalism has rekindled war in parts of Eastern Europe.

This should not be surprising. Where peoples are deeply commingled, the project of constructing states on the basis of ethnic identity is a recipe for disaster. The collapse of multinational states has triggered the erection of barriers between their former subjects. The rise of democracy in formerly tyrannous regimes has led to the attempt to establish ethnically homogeneous states.

The connection between the rise of democracy and the break-up of multinational states is not accidental. Democracy demands trust. Where there are ethnic groups with a history of mutual enmity, trust may be slight, or lacking. If they form what looks like being a permanent minority, ethnic groups may fear being permanent losers from democratic decision-making. Seceding in order to form a separate state in which they are no longer a minority may seem an answer to their fears, but it is likely to provoke a parallel response from the existing majority. In such circumstances, democracy and ethnic cleansing go together.

This interaction shows up a danger of democracy, particularly in its more participatory varieties. As its advocates have long recognized, republican democracy can be realized in small, culturally homogeneous communities.[19] Rousseau understood that if his ideal of self-government was practically workable anywhere it was only in states no larger, and no less homogeneous, than ancient Athens or Renaissance Florence.

The implication of Rousseau's insight for us is the opposite of that which he intended. In our circumstances, democracy cannot mean self-government by nations or peoples. Rousseau's ideal of democracy is the collective self-rule of a single community. When society contains several ways of life, that ideal is unachievable, and its pursuit dangerous.

Where nations or peoples are interwoven in plural societies, republican democracy is a prescription for division. It encourages the break-up of large plural societies and states, and necessitates the construction of small ethnic nation-states. The end-result can only be partition and a continuing risk of war. This is an objection not only to Rousseau's ideal of democracy, but to all republican views, including Machiavelli's.

It is better to detach democracy from ideas of national self-determination, and think of it as a means whereby disparate communities can reach common decisions. In a growing number of contexts, democracy and the nation-state are no longer coterminous – if only because the boundaries and composition of nation-states are contested. Yet there are few examples of stable democratic government in multinational states.

Beyond Europe, the nation-state has rarely taken deep root. True, in their quite different ways, Japan and the United States are classical nation-states. Again, though it is far from having a modern state, China is engaged in an ambitious project of nation-building. Yet again, South Africa has embarked on the enterprise of forging a single national culture from a mosaic of ethnic loyalties. The age of nation-building is far from being over.

Even so, there are many countries that are unlikely ever to have a common national culture, or in which it has begun unmistakably to unravel. Russia is a relic of empire rather than any kind of nation-state, and the Balkans are strewn with the ruins of multinational states. Turkey inherits an uncompromising modernist state from the Ataturkist era, but it is divided between secular and Islamist ways of life and faces serious problems with national minorities. Indonesia continues to claim to be a nation-state, but the very idea of Indonesian nationhood is rejected by separatist movements, one of which – East Timor – has succeeded in gaining independence. India and Israel are increasingly divided on religious and ethnic lines. In all of these countries, the model of the European nation-state has a weakening hold, or has led to a process of political fragmentation that has no obvious end-point.

It is a mistake to look for a single successor to the modern nation-state. Late modern circumstances are too diverse. Not only the forms but the internal structures of legitimate states vary widely. In some circumstances, devolution and federal institutions may be useful devices. When they are territorially separable, parcelling out in different legislative bodies the power to make common decisions can help reduce conflict between communities.

There will always be differences about the division of powers and about where borders should be set. In some cases – in Quebec, Catalonia and Scotland, say – these are not so deep as to endanger the settlement that has been reached on federalism or devolution. In other circumstances, they are so bitter that secession or partition may be the only practicable solution. It may seem ironic to include partition among devices for fostering peaceful coexistence. Still, in Cyprus and India, partition has allowed a form of coexistence in circumstances where peace had once not been an option. The same may be true in parts of the Balkans.

Federalism is not a panacea. Where it can be achieved, its human cost may be enormous. American federalism, which is often held up as a model, was founded on one of the most savage civil wars of modern times.[20]

Another device is consociationalism. A consociational regime is one in which communities, not individuals, are bearers of many important rights. In consociational systems, each community has institutions of its own, in which its own values and laws are authoritative, while sharing a common framework with the rest. As devices for enabling different ways of life to cohabit in the same territory, consociational institutions have much to be said for them. Unfortunately, if they rest solely on agreements among their component communities, they are rarely stable for long.

Where different communities are commingled in the same territory, consociational institutions allow each to maintain a separate identity while interacting to mutual benefit with the rest. The Ottoman Empire can be seen as a consociational regime, while Lebanon, Belgium, and Northern Ireland after the peace agreement, all display some consociational features.

Where a territory contains several clearly demarcated communities or ways of life whose demands for political and legal recognition cannot all be met, consociational institutions have a number of advantages. They make possible a form of democratic government that does not presuppose a single common culture. Provided there is sufficient allegiance to a common framework, consociational systems allow the values of different cultures to be reflected in parallel jurisdictions. By decoupling legal jurisdiction from territorial sovereignty, consociational regimes enable different ways of life to cohabit, without relegating their distinctive values to the private sphere. Thereby they allow full legal recognition to several common identities.

Consociational regimes confer rights on communities rather than (or as well as) individuals. Where ways of life have long been interwoven, consociational institutions are defensible only insofar as they protect the interests of people of hybrid identity. When communities or ways of life are fluid and permeable, they are not easily individuated. When many people belong to several ways of life, it makes no sense to make ways of life the primary bearers of rights.

In such circumstances, consociational institutions may still be useful as ways in which collective identities can be embodied, but they are likely to be embedded in a common framework which rests partly or largely on individual rights. Switzerland and the Netherlands are examples of long-standing liberal regimes which incorporate some consociational institutions.

The most serious disadvantage of consociational systems is that they are often unstable. The evidence of history is that consociational regimes which depend mainly on negotiations among their respective communities are usually short-lived. They do not survive for long unless they are underwritten by an external power.

Diplomatic and military intervention in the Balkans came about because establishing nation-states on the European civic model has proved impossible and attempts to establish ethnically homogeneous nation-states have occasioned gross violations of rudimentary human rights. The upshot in parts of former Yugoslavia has been the establishment of a number of more or less consociational regimes whose stability has been guaranteed from outside, by the powers which installed them.[21]

The regimes that have been established in Bosnia and Kosovo are hybrids – part liberal, part consociational and partly involving *de facto* partitions. The most important feature of these hybrid forms of governance is that they do not depend on consent. They are protectorates, whose security is guaranteed by the powers which established them.

Like that which prevailed under its Ottoman rulers, the peace that has been imposed in the Balkans rests on a foundation less uncertain than agreements among the various communities who are its beneficiaries. What we are witnessing in the Balkans at the turn of the twenty-first century may prove to be the reinvention of the institution of empire as a remedy for the evils that flow from the attempt to construct ethnic nation-states. Yet it is far from clear that the imperial institutions that are under construction can recreate multi-ethnic societies.

In the very different circumstances of contemporary South Africa, democratic institutions have been established as part of an enterprise of constructing a modern nation-state. The obstacles are daunting. The pervasive inheritance of apartheid has resulted in high levels of economic inequality and a low level of civil order, together with many-sided ethnic divisions. These conditions make a collapse or fragmentation of the state a real possibility. Yet there is no solution in separatism. The country's populations have long been too commingled for that to be feasible. There is no alternative to the wager on nation-building that is presently underway. The fate of South Africa depends on whether a national culture can be built that contains and transcends ethnic loyalties.

In much of the Balkans, peace, democracy and a multi-ethnic society may not be achievable together. Liberal thought has repressed the painful fact that these goals are not always compatible. As a result, it has little to say about how their conflicts can be managed. The decline of the classical nation-state and the spread of democratic institutions have engendered a set of questions to which the standard varieties of liberal thought contain few answers. Political leaders and policy-makers have been driven to improvise institutions for peaceful coexistence among warring communities in circumstances in which existing political theories offer little useful guidance. One of the reasons why liberal thought no longer gives much guidance to practice is that it takes the modern state for granted. In much of the world today, however, there is nothing that resembles a modern state. Some countries remain strongly governed. Western Europe, North America and Japan retain highly effective states. Elsewhere, in much of the former Soviet Union, in Africa, the Balkans, southern Asia and parts of Latin America, the state has collapsed, or else become deeply corroded. In these regions, the state has lost the control over organized violence that has defined it since the beginning of the modern period.[22]

In countries where modern government has crumbled away, anarchy rather than tyranny has become the chief threat to human rights. In these countries the worst crimes against humanity are no longer the work of states. They are committed by irregular militias, political organizations or criminal cartels, over which no state has much effective control.

Twentieth-century liberal thought viewed states as the worst violators of human rights, and with good reason. In the absence of technologically advanced, strongly governed states, the Holocaust and the Gulag could not have occurred. Most twentieth-century crimes against humanity were the work of states. Today that is ceasing to be true.

The re-emergence of anarchy as the chief threat to human freedom and well-being in many parts of the world poses questions that recent liberal thought is ill equipped to answer. For much of its history liberalism was an enterprise of state-building. In the fragility of the state our time resembles the late medieval and early modern eras more than it does the last two hundred years. Yet liberal thinkers seem not to have noticed the corrosion of the state that has occurred in many parts of the world.

One reason for this lacuna in recent liberal thought is its legalism. Current orthodoxies treat the rule of law as an accomplished fact. By passing over the political conditions that make the rule of law possible, the legalist liberalism that has prevailed over the past generation has been able to represent law as a free-standing institution. It has contrived to disregard the fact that the institution of law always depends on the power of the state.

The most important reason for the neglect by many contemporary liberal thinkers of the erosion of state power is that it allows moral and political conflicts to be suppressed or evaded. A condition of anarchy makes rivalry among rights impossible to avoid. Where there is a risk of pogroms against minorities, it may be impossible to respect rights of free speech or assembly fully. Where there is a recent history of division among communities with distinct religious traditions, unqualified freedom of religion may be a prelude to renewed conflict.

Anarchy illuminates the fact that justice is an artefact of enforcement. Where there is anarchy, there are no rights. As Hobbes put it: 'Where there is no common power, there is no law: where no law, no injustice. Force, and fraud, are in war the two cardinal virtues.'[23] Justice and rights are conventions, upheld – in the last resort – by force. This is a truth that recent liberal philosophy has found it convenient to forget.

The first condition of the protection of human rights is an effective modern state. Without the power of enforcement, there are no rights, and any kind of commodious living is an impossibility.[24] For most of humankind, the worst threat to freedom today is not an overmighty state. It is anarchy. In consequence, it is not Rawls or Hayek that we have most to learn from, nor even John Stuart Mill, but Hobbes.

There is much in Hobbes's thought that is mistaken or anachronistic. Hobbes believed that life without a common power was a struggle among individuals for safety and pre-eminence. In this he was mistaken. When states fail it is communities, not individuals, that wage war with one another.[25]

Hobbes's view of the state is unnecessarily absolutist. His view that an effective state cannot allow rights to its subjects (beyond the right to self-preservation, which they can never give up) is not supported by history. Nor is his assertion of unqualified sovereignty in the relations of states with one another.

Hobbes's rationalistic apparatus of social contract is not only redundant. It is misconceived in trying to show that one human interest can defeat all others. Hobbes is right in thinking that the endemic threat of violent death is an evil that stands in the way of any kind of worthwhile human life; but it surely cannot be the only such evil, or one that is bound to override all others. If, as Hobbes thought, there is no *summum bonum*, neither can there be a *summum malum*.

Yet, despite the fact that he was himself the opposite of any kind of pluralist, Hobbes's conception of politics can be reformulated in pluralist terms. The end of politics is not the mere absence of war, but a *modus vivendi* among goods and evils. Like a Hobbesian peace, this can never be achieved once and for all.

Amended in this way, Hobbes's thought implies that the most important feature of any regime is not how far it succeeds in promoting any particular value. It is how well it enables conflicts among values to be negotiated. The test of legitimacy for any regime is its success in mediating conflicts of values – including rival ideals of justice.

When we are applying this test, the trundling distinction between *de facto* and *de jure* authority is less than helpful. It runs parallel with the demarcation of reasons of principle from reasons of prudence that is so dear to liberal thinkers who take their bearings from Kant. Such force as this venerable distinction possesses derives from the illusive notions that 'morality' designates an especially potent kind of value that always overrides every other and that what 'morality' demands is normally self-evident to reasonable people.

In practice, 'morality' and 'prudence' are not so easily parted, and it is often very hard to know what is right. Ethical life is commonly a shifting compromise among ideals, reached in part by prudential reasoning. In government, legitimacy invariably arises from settlements involving an accommodation of interests.

In ethics and politics, we pursue compromises amongst incompatible claims. We seek compromise rather than consistency because consistency cannot be achieved without impoverishing our lives. There are better and worse compromises, and some that are thoroughly bad; but what all have in common is that they involve reaching an accommodation among opposed ideals and interests. If such accommodations are condemned by 'morality', so much the worse for 'morality'.

In a neo-Hobbesian view, one regime is more legitimate than another if it is more successful in facilitating, and delivering, such compromises. No one type of regime, liberal or otherwise, is likely to be better than all others in this respect, and none is bound to be.

In some ways, the neo-Hobbesian conception I have outlined resembles the political liberalism advocated by John Rawls. Like the Rawlsian theory, *modus vivendi* affirms that the test of legitimacy for any regime is not its conformity with any comprehensive conception of the good. At the same time, it denies that conformity with a theory of justice can be the test of legitimacy either. For, as I have shown, no theory of justice of the kind attempted by Rawls can cope with conflicts among basic liberties.

Again, *modus vivendi* is like justice as fairness in recognizing that no regime which attempts to impose a single view of the good on society can hope to be legitimate in a circumstance of pluralism. Where *modus vivendi* differs from Rawls's theory is in its recognition that justice cannot be insulated from conflicts of value arising from rival conceptions of the good.

Yet again, the Rawlsian view and the neo-Hobbesian view are alike in acknowledging that in the absence of some goods a worthwhile human life is scarcely possible. But, like classical natural law theories, the Rawlsian view depends on primary goods being chain-linked with one another. In contrast, the neo-Hobbesian view recognizes that, though it is true that some primary goods may reinforce one another, nothing guarantees this happy result.

In fact, competition among the primary goods of social life is endemic. In consequence, human rights and liberties do not compose anything resembling a consistent, harmonious system, nor are they indivisible. Forever at war with one another, they are almost infinitely divisible. Whereas the Rawlsian claim that primary goods do not conflict with one another is contrary to experience, the Hobbesian view has the advantage of being faithful to ethical and political life.[26]

Despite their similarities, the neo-Hobbesian view and the Rawlsian view exemplify rival projects. Following Kant, Rawls seeks to formulate principles of justice which any reasonable person is bound to accept, or at any rate cannot reject, regardless of her conception of the good. The result is a liberal philosophy of right in which justice is meant to have priority over all other goods. Following Hobbes, the account of *modus vivendi* I have defended does not aim to prescribe principles of right that are independent of particular conceptions of the good. Instead it judges regimes in terms of their capacity to mediate compromises among rival views of the good. The result is a liberal philosophy in which the good has priority over the right, but in which no one view of the good has overall priority over all others.

Insofar as liberalism is the project of an ideal regime, it is defeated by conflicts of value. That is the core of the argument for turning from that view of the liberal project to one in which the pursuit of *modus vivendi* is central. Yet value-pluralism does not strictly entail *modus vivendi*. As a matter of logic, value-pluralism cannot entail any political project.

All that value-pluralism implies is that strongly universalist moralities – religious or political – are illusions. As it is commonly interpreted, liberalism is just such a highly universalist morality in that it holds that one and only one regime can be fully legitimate. If value-pluralism tends to undermine such universalist claims, it cannot at the same time show peaceful coexistence to be a universal imperative.

The case for *modus vivendi* is not that it is some kind of transcendent value which all ways of life are bound to honour. It is that all or nearly all ways of life have interests that make peaceful coexistence worth pursuing. Peaceful coexistence is worth pursuing only insofar as it advances human interests. Like any political ideal, it is a contingent good. This is not a peculiar disability of *modus vivendi*. It is a limitation of all forms of ethical reasoning. No ethical argument has force unless it latches on to reasons for action that human agents have already.

That does not mean that only ways of life which already accept an ideal of toleration have reason to seek *modus vivendi*. *Modus vivendi* is desirable not only for ways of life that acknowledge the value of toleration, but also for those that do not. A way of life that shared no interests with any other would have no interest in *modus vivendi*. Such ways of life are rare, if they are not non-existent. Because they are practised by human beings, all ways of life have some interests in common. As we all know, it is frequently those interests that divide us. At the same time they give us reason to pursue coexistence.

The reasons that move communities to seek coexistence with one another are many and varied – no less so than human interests. The variety of interests that lead people to seek an accommodation with one another is what makes peaceful coexistence possible. It is foolish to imagine that society or government is at its most stable when it rests on foundations of principle. Often, it is principled commitment to rival ideals that makes peaceful coexistence impossible.

For all its talk of pluralism, the liberal political philosophy that has been dominant over the past generation thinks of conflicts of value as if they were a passing phase in human affairs. In contrast, *modus vivendi* is a view that takes rival views of the good and the right to be a universal feature of political life. Now and in any future we can envision, communities and states will be divided by rival claims about justice and what makes human life worth living.

Unlike liberal toleration, *modus vivendi* does not cherish the hope that the world will someday converge on truth. It does not seek convergence on the truth – even the truth of value-pluralism. The idea that political life could be without illusions is itself illusive. Nor, if it were possible, would politics without illusions be without loss. As Nietzsche perceived,[27] illusion may be a condition of some forms of life that are worth living. If variety in ways of life depends partly on some of them making strongly universalist claims, a world in which everyone subscribed to value-pluralism might not be notably diverse. In that case, value-pluralism could be self-undermining.

The theory of *modus vivendi* does not imagine that a world

without illusions is possible, or wholly desirable. It seeks only to cure us of the false hopes that go with philosophies that promise an end to conflicts of value. In our time, an hubristic species of rights-based liberalism is foremost among those philosophies.

It may seem that giving up this liberal philosophy and opting for *modus vivendi* involves giving up liberalism itself. From one perspective this must be so. *Modus vivendi* relinquishes the project of a universal regime. If that is the essence of liberalism, then *modus vivendi* cannot be other than a post-liberal philosophy.[28]

All varieties of liberalism which advance a strongly universalist morality are versions of the Enlightenment project. In part, these species of liberalism rest on a positivist philosophy of history. History has falsified that philosophy. In part, also, they embody the rationalist ideal of reconstructing ethical life so as to resolve conflicts of value by applying 'principles'. That ideal runs aground on the fact that these 'principles' turn out to be either themselves conflicting, or else too indeterminate to be able to guide practice.

It cannot be denied that Enlightenment universalism is a powerful tendency in liberal philosophy. It marks the thought even of thinkers, such as Hobbes and Hume, who did not subscribe to the ideal of a universal regime. For much of its history, liberalism and the project of a universal rational morality have been indistinguishable. All liberal philosophies that take their cue from Locke or Kant, or which embody the side of John Stuart Mill's thought that aimed for a reconstructed version of Benthamite utilitarianism, are variations on the Enlightenment project of a rationally reconstructed, universally authoritative morality. Not only Rawls and Nozick but Popper and Hayek are disciples of this philosophy of liberal universalism. If anything has become clear in the present inquiry, it is that *this* liberal philosophy is a dead letter.

For those who think liberalism and the Enlightenment project inseparable, this can only be a defeat for liberalism. But there is another way of thinking that is no less coeval with liberal thought. This other liberalism is much less closely tied to Enlightenment hopes.

We can think of the liberal project not as aiming to found a universal regime or way of life but as the pursuit of *modus vivendi* among different regimes and ways of life. If we think of it in this way, liberalism is not a partisan claim for the universal authority of a particular morality, but the search for terms of coexistence between different moralities. In this alternative view, liberalism has to do with handling the conflicts of cultures that will always be different, not founding a universal civilization.

Adopting *modus vivendi* as the core of the liberal project means that liberalism can no longer be identified with particular values – be they the values that are supposed to be summarized in theories of justice, or those that go with the way of life of autonomous individuals. But there are limits on what can count as *modus vivendi*.

As we have seen, there is a coherent view of human rights in which they provide protection against evils that forestall anything recognizable as a worthwhile human life. From this standpoint, human rights are constraints on the pursuit of coexistence. From another, they frame its terms. Either way, rights do not give the deliverance from conflict and choice for which liberal universalists yearn. Whatever our view of human rights, we will face dilemmas to which there is no solution that does not contain wrong.

Adopting *modus vivendi* involves relinquishing some liberal hopes. At the same time, it resolves an incoherence in liberalism that has been with it from the start. The claims of liberalism as a system of universal principles were never defensible. Today, when reconciling different ways of life to the fact of their coexistence is an urgent task nearly everywhere, they have become harmful.

Neither of the rival philosophies can claim to be quintessentially liberal. Both are found among liberal thinkers – sometimes, as in the case of John Stuart Mill, in the same liberal thinker. In recent times, the liberalism of rational consensus has gone virtually unchallenged. In their very different ways, thinkers such as Isaiah Berlin and Michael Oakeshott have upheld another liberal philosophy that is not tethered to ideas of consensus and rational choice, but they have been on the margins. The mainstream of liberal philosophy has continued to be animated by Enlightenment hopes that have long since become anachronistic.

In political philosophy there are few timeless verities. Both Rawlsian and neo-Hobbesian liberalism are responses to modern pluralism. Rawlsian liberalism seeks to transcend pluralism by developing an agreed conception of justice. In so doing it reposes extravagant hopes in the overlapping consensus which it imagines it has found in some late modern societies. As a consequence, its real aim is the restoration of a non-existent or vanishing ethical monoculture. By contrast, the neo-Hobbesian philosophy of *modus vivendi* is well suited to societies, now and in the future, that contain many ways of life.

The task of political philosophy is not to give practice a foundation. It has never had one in the past, yet somehow the human species has stumbled on The aim of political philosophy is to return to practice with fewer illusions. For us, this means shedding the illusion that theories of justice and rights can deliver us from the ironies and tragedies of politics.

For some this may seem too sceptical a conclusion. It would be idle to deny that *modus vivendi* is a sceptical view. But what it gives up is not the belief that we can know the difference between right and wrong. It is the traditional faith, which contemporary liberal orthodoxy has inherited, that questions of value can have only one right answer. To relinquish this is no loss, since it means that the diversity of ways of life and regimes is a mark of human freedom, not of error.

Liberal toleration sought to temper rival universal claims about the good with an ideal of reasonable disagreement; but it never gave up the hope of rational consensus on the best way of life for humankind. *Modus vivendi* continues the liberal search for peaceful coexistence; but it does so by giving up the belief that one way of life, or a single type of regime, could be best for all.

Notes

Chapter 1   Liberal Toleration

1   The pervasive dependency of Locke's political thought on a particular version of the Christian religion has been shown in John Dunn's classic study *The Political Thought of John Locke: An Historical Account of the Argument of the 'Two Treatises of Government'*, Cambridge, Cambridge University Press, 1969.

2   For an interpretation of Hobbes as a thinker who returns to a pagan tradition in which it is not belief but practice which is primary, see Michael Oakeshott, *Hobbes on Civil Association*, Oxford, Blackwell, 1975, pp. 69–72.

3   Voltaire, *Philosophical Dictionary*, London, J. and H.L. Hunt, 1824, vol. VI, 'Toleration', p. 272.

4   See Alasdair MacIntyre: *After Virtue: A Study in Moral Theory*, London, Duckworth, 1981; *Whose Justice? Which Rationality?*, London, Duckworth, 1988; *Three Rival Versions of Moral Enquiry*, London, Duckworth, 1990; *Dependent Rational Animals: Why Human Beings Need the Virtues*, London, Duckworth, 1999.

5   I have considered the inadequacies of Hayek's treatment of social justice in my *Hayek on Liberty*, Third Edition, London and New York, Routledge, 1998, 'Postscript: Hayek and the Dissolution of Classical Liberalism', pp. 146–61.

6   On the anti-political character of Rawlsian liberalism, see 'Rawls's Anti-political Liberalism', in my *Endgames: Questions*

in Late Modern Political Thought, Cambridge, Polity Press, 1997, pp. 51–4.

7 I noted the continuation in his later work of Rawls's early agenda regarding the strong determinacy and finality of his principles of justice in 'Contractarian Method, Private Property and the Market Economy', in my *Liberalisms: Essays in Political Philosophy,* London and New York, Routledge, 1989, pp. 161–98.

8 The early Robert Nozick may be taken as a spokesman of the view that market freedoms are derivations from fundamental human rights. See Robert Nozick, *Anarchy, State and Utopia,* Oxford and New York, Basil Blackwell, 1974.

9 For an argument against both egalitarian and libertarian versions of liberal legalism, see my *Beyond the New Right: Markets, Government and the Common Environment,* London and New York, Routledge, 1993, pp. 76–92. For an argument that market institutions best advance personal autonomy when they are complemented by enabling welfare institutions, see ibid., pp. 99–110.

10 For a statement of Rawls's views that may be definitive, see John Rawls, *Collected Papers,* ed. Samuel Freeman, Cambridge, Mass., and London, Harvard University Press, 1999.

11 I am indebted to Dr Henry Hardy for conversation on the conflict between value-pluralism and the claims of universal religions.

12 For a critique of social democracy from the standpoint of value-pluralism, see 'After Social Democracy', in my *Endgames,* pp. 11–50.

13 For a thoughtful contrary view, see Richard Rorty, *Contingency, Irony and Solidarity,* Cambridge, Cambridge University Press, 1989, especially chs 3 and 4, and *Truth and Progress: Philosophical Papers,* Cambridge, Cambridge University Press, 1998, particularly chs 9 and 10.

14 Stuart Hampshire, 'Justice is Strife', *Proceedings and Addresses of the American Philosophical Association,* vol. 65, no. 3, November 1991, pp. 24–5.

15 On the contemporary cult of the free market, see my *False Dawn: The Delusions of Global Capitalism,* London and New York, Granta Books and the New Press, 1998.

16 For an argument that much in the Enlightenment is a secularization of Christian hopes, see my *Enlightenment's Wake: Politics and Culture at the Close of the Modern Age,* London and New York, Routledge, 1995, ch. 10.

17   I consider some of the difficulties of defining and delimiting the liberal tradition in the Postscript to the Second Edition of my *Liberalism*, Buckingham, Open University Press, 1995.

18   See F.A. Hayek, *The Constitution of Liberty*, Chicago, Henry Regnery Company, 1960, pp. 174ff. For a statement of a view antithetical to Hayek's that is relevant today, despite having been first published in 1911, see L.T. Hobhouse, *Liberalism*, New York, Oxford University Press, 1964.

19   An invaluable account of the new Pyrrhonism is to be found in Richard H. Popkin's *The History of Scepticism from Erasmus to Spinoza*, Fourth Edition, Berkeley, University of California Press, 1979. See also Popkin's *The High Road to Pyrrhonism*, ed. R.A. Watson and J.E. Force, Indianapolis and Cambridge, Hackett Publishing Co., 1980.

20   Hayek, *The Constitution of Liberty*, p. 56.

21   For an admirable recent study of Smith that does full justice to the subtlety and complexity of his thought, see Charles L. Griswold, Jr, *Adam Smith and the Virtues of Enlightenment*, Cambridge, Cambridge University Press, 1999. For a study of Smith's highly complex relations with 'liberalism', see Donald Winch, *Adam Smith's Politics*, Cambridge, Cambridge University Press, 1978.

22   See James Fitzjames Stephen, *Liberty, Equality, Fraternity*, ed. Stuart D. Warner, Indianapolis, Liberty Fund, 1993.

23   See Oakeshott, *Hobbes on Civil Association*, p. 63. For two other distinguished interpretations of Hobbes as one of the chief authors of the liberal tradition, see Leo Strauss, *The Political Philosophy of Thomas Hobbes*, Chicago, University of Chicago Press, 1952, and C.B. Macpherson, *The Political Theory of Possessive Individualism*, Oxford, Clarendon Press, 1962.

      Two more recent studies in which Hobbes appears as a proto-liberal are Gregory S. Kavka, *Hobbesian Moral and Political Theory*, Princeton, NJ, Princeton University Press, 1986, and Jean Hampton, *Hobbes and the Social Contract Tradition*, Cambridge, Cambridge University Press, 1986.

24   For a powerful and highly original intepretation of Hume as a philosopher of common life, see Donald W. Livingstone, *Hume's Philosophy of Common Life*, Chicago, University of Chicago Press, 1984.

      I considered the relations of Pyrrhonism with politics in 'After Liberalism', the Postscript to my *Liberalisms*, pp. 261–4.

25   On the emergence of Romanticism, see Isaiah Berlin, *The Roots*

of Romanticism, ed. Henry Hardy, London, Chatto and Windus, 1999, especially chs 2 and 3.

26 See Wilhelm von Humboldt, *The Limits of State Action*, ed. J.W. Burrow, Indianapolis, Liberty Fund, 1993. John Burrow's Introduction (pp.xvii–lviii) is itself a notable contribution to thought on liberalism.

27 J.S. Mill, *On Liberty and Other Essays*, ed. John Gray, Oxford, Oxford University Press, 1998, pp. 69–70.

28 I have discussed some of the tensions in Mill's thought in the Postscript to the Second Edition of my book, *Mill on Liberty: A Defence*, London and New York, Routledge, 1996, pp. 130–58.

29 For Mill's arguments against the illiberal tendencies in French positivism, see his *Auguste Comte and Positivism*, Ann Arbor, University of Michigan Press, 1973. A useful selection from *Auguste Comte and Positivism* can be found in John Stuart Mill, *Utilitarianism, On Liberty and Considerations on Representative Government*, ed. H.B. Acton, London, J.M. Dent and Sons, 1972, pp. 395–413.

30 See 'John Stuart Mill and the Ends of Life', in Isaiah Berlin, *Four Essays on Liberty*, Oxford, Oxford University Press, 1969, p. 188.

31 I discuss Berlin's agonistic liberalism in my *Isaiah Berlin*, London and Princeton, NJ, HarperCollins and Princeton University Press, 1996, ch. 6.

32 Michael Oakeshott, *Rationalism in Politics and other Essays*, London and New York, Methuen, p. 136.

33 Mill, *On Liberty and Other Essays*, pp. 13–14.

34 I argued that Oakeshott's thought issues in an ideal of *modus vivendi* in 'Oakeshott on Law, Liberty and Civil Association' in *Liberalisms*, pp.199–216. I advanced an interpretation of Oakeshott as a liberal thinker in 'Oakeshott as a Liberal', in my *Post-liberalism: Studies in Political Thought*, London and New York, Routledge, 1993, ch. 4.

A similar interpretation of Oakeshott is presented by Wendell John Coats, Jr, 'Michael Oakeshott as Liberal Theorist', *Canadian Journal of Political Science*, vol. XVIII, no. 4, December 1985, pp. 773–87. I owe this reference to Oakeshott, who expressed his admiration of Coats's paper in conversation with me.

I discuss some affinities and contrasts between Oakeshott and Berlin in 'Berlin, Oakeshott and Enlightenment' in my *Endgames*, pp. 84–96.

Chapter 2   Plural Values

1   The extended philosophical literature on value-pluralism does
    not contain any consensus on the meaning of incommensura-
    bility. My understanding of it may not correspond to that which
    is found in some sections of the literature. The account of plu-
    ral values I advance is indebted to the work of others; but it
    does not claim to be based on them.

    I am indebted most particularly to the work of Isaiah Berlin,
    of which an admirable selection can be found in *The Proper
    Study of Mankind*, ed. Henry Hardy and Roger Hausheer, Lon-
    don, Chatto and Windus, 1997. I offer an interpretation and
    assessment of Berlin's value-pluralism and its relations with lib-
    eralism in my *Isaiah Berlin*, London and Princeton, NJ,
    HarperCollins and Princeton University Press, 1996.

    I am also deeply indebted to Joseph Raz, particularly to his
    The Morality of Freedom, Oxford, Clarendon Press, 1986; ' Fa-
    cing Up: A Reply', *Southern California Law Review*, vol. 62,
    nos 3 and 4, March–May 1989, pp. 1153–235; and *Ethics in the
    Public Domain: Essays in the Morality of Law and Politics*, Ox-
    ford, Clarendon Press, 1994.

    I have learnt much from Stuart Hampshire: *Thought and Ac-
    tion*, London, Chatto and Windus, 1959; *Freedom of Mind and
    Other Essays*, Oxford, Clarendon Press, 1972; *Morality and
    Conflict*, Oxford, Basil Blackwell, 1983; *Innocence and Experi-
    ence*, Allen Lane / The Penguin Press, 1989; and 'Justice is Strife',
    Proceedings and Addresses of the American Philosophical Association,
    vol. 65, no. 3, November 1991, pp. 19–27; Bernard Williams:
    Problems of the Self, Cambridge, Cambridge University Press,
    1973; *Moral Luck*, Cambridge, Cambridge University Press, 1981;
    Ethics and the Limits of Philosophy, London, Collins, 1985; and
    Shame and Necessity, Berkeley, Calif., University of California
    Press, 1993; H.L.A. Hart: *Essays in Jurisprudence and Philoso-
    phy*, Oxford, Clarendon Press, 1983; P.F. Strawson: 'Individual
    Morality and Social Ideal', in *Freedom and Resentment*, Lon-
    don, Methuen, 1974; and 'Morality and Perception', in *Scepti-
    cism and Naturalism: Some Varieties*, London, Methuen, 1985;
    Richard Wollheim: 'The Sheep and the Ceremony', in his *The
    Mind and Its Depths*, Cambridge, Mass., and London, Harvard
    University Press, 1993, pp. 1–21; and Avishai Margalit: *The
    Decent Society*, Cambridge, Mass., and London, Harvard Uni-

versity Press, 1996.

Helpful discussions of the issues raised by value-pluralism can be found in Michael Stocker, *Plural and Conflicting Values*, Oxford, Clarendon Press, 1990; John Kekes, *The Morality of Pluralism*, Princeton, NJ, Princeton University Press, 1993; and Charles Larmore, *Patterns of Moral Complexity*, Cambridge, Cambridge University Press, 1987, and *The Morals of Modernity*, Cambridge, Cambridge University Press, 1996. John Casey's *Pagan Virtue: An Essay in Ethics*, Oxford, Oxford University Press, 1990, contains some illuminating thoughts on the incommensurability of pagan and Christian values.

A useful survey of recent work on value-pluralism may be found in *Incommensurability, Incomparability and Practical Reason*, Ruth Chang, ed., Cambridge, Mass., and London, Harvard University Press, 1997; the papers by Raz, Wiggins and Griffin are particularly notable.

A valuable examination of value-pluralism in its relations with recent political philosophy may be found in Glen Newey, 'Value-pluralism in Contemporary Liberalism', *Dialogue*, no. XXXVII, 1998, pp. 493–552. Other useful discussions are: C.J. McKnight, 'Pluralism, Realism and Truth', and John Skorupski, 'Value-Pluralism', in David Archard, ed., *Philosophy and Pluralism*, Cambridge, Cambridge University Press, 1996, pp. 87–100 and 101–16, respectively; S. Gardbaum, 'Liberalism, Autonomy and Moral Conflict', *Stanford Law Review*, vol. 48, no. 2, January 1996, pp. 385–417; Steven Lukes, *Times Literary Supplement*, 27 March 1998; John Horton, 'The Politics of value-pluralism', *Keele University Research Paper 22*, 1997; Richard Bellamy, *Liberalism and Pluralism: Towards a Politics of Compromise*, London and New York, Routledge, 1999; and John Skorupski, *Ethical Explorations*, Oxford, OUP, 1999.

An interesting dialogue on Berlin's value-pluralism may be found in Gerald C. MacCallum, Jr, 'Berlin on the Compatibility of Values, Ideals and "Ends"', *Ethics*, no. LXXVII, 1967, pp. 139–45, and G.A. Cohen, 'A Note on Values and Sacrifices', *Ethics*, 1969, pp. 159–62.

A memorable exchange on the relations of value-pluralism with liberalism occurs between George D. Crowder, 'Pluralism and Liberalism', and Isaiah Berlin and Bernard Williams, 'Pluralism and Liberalism: A Reply', *Political Studies*, vol. 42, no. 2, June 1994, pp. 293–309. See also George D. Crowder, 'From Value-pluralism to Liberalism', *Critical Review of Inter-*

national Social and Political Philosophy, vol. 1, no. 3, 1998, pp. 2–17.

I am indebted to Hubert Dreyfus and Charles Spinosa for writings and conversation which stimulated me to pursue links between pluralism and realism in Heidegger's account of science and in ethics. For an account of Heidegger's plural realism, see Hubert Dreyfus, *Being in the World: A Commentary on Heidegger's 'Being and Time', Division 1*, Cambridge, Mass. and London, MIT Press, 1991, especially pp. 251–65. For a general discussion of plural realism in science, see Charles Spinosa and Hubert Dreyfus, 'Two Kinds of Antiessentialism and their Consequences', *Critical Inquiry*, no. 22, Summer 1996, pp. 735–63.

Interpretations of realism in some ways parallel to those of Dreyfus's Heidegger may be derived from Wittgenstein's *Philosophical Investigations*, tr. G.E.M. Anscombe, Oxford, Basil Blackwell, 1953, *Remarks on the Foundations of Mathematics*, tr. G.E.M. Anscombe, ed. G.H. von Wright, Rush Rhees and G.E.M. Anscombe, Oxford, Basil Blackwell, 1967, and *On Certainty*, ed. G.E.M. Anscombe and G.H. von Wright, Oxford, Basil Blackwell, 1969.

I have also benefited from discussions of realism and incommensurability in Nelson Goodman, *Languages of Art*, Indianapolis, Hackett Publishing Co., 1976, and *Ways of Worldmaking*, Indianapolis, Hackett Publishing Co., 1978; Thomas Kuhn, 'Afterwords', in Paul Horwich, ed., *World Changes: Thomas Kuhn and the Nature of Science*, Cambridge, Mass., MIT Press, 1993; and Richard Rorty, *Truth and Progress: Philosophical Papers*, Cambridge, Cambridge University Press, 1998.

2 Raz, *The Morality of Freedom*, p. 352.
3 For an illuminating discussion of Aristotle's views on conflicts of value, see Stocker, *Plural and Conflicting Values*, especially chs 3 and 7.
4 Bruno Snell, *The Discovery of Mind: The Greek Origins of European Thought*, New York and Evanston, Ill., Harper and Row, 1953, p. 159.
5 Raz, *The Morality of Freedom*, p. 396.
6 Isaiah Berlin, 'Two Concepts of Liberty', in *The Proper Study of Mankind*, pp. 238, 240.
7 Wittgenstein, *Philosophical Investigations*, p. 88, § 242.
8 The story was told me by Isaiah Berlin from what I take to be personal knowledge.

9   Michael Oakeshott, 'Rationalism in Politics: A Reply to Professor Raphael', *Political Studies*, February 1965, p. 90.

10 For a well-rehearsed argument against the possibility of incommensurable values, see James Griffin, 'Incommensurability: What's the Problem?', in Chang, ed., *Incommensurability, Incomparability and Practical Reason*, pp. 35–51.

11 For a different account of the idea of a conceptual scheme, see Donald Davidson, 'On the Very Idea of a Conceptual Scheme', in *Inquiries into Truth and Interpretation*, Oxford, Oxford University Press, 1984, pp. 183–98.

12 See Michael N. Forster, *Hegel's Idea of a Phenomenology of Spirit*, Chicago, University of Chicago Press, 1998, for some forceful criticisms of the view that radically different conceptual schemes cannot exist. I am indebted to Charles Spinosa for drawing Forster's discussion to my attention.

13 J.L. Austin, *A Plea for Excuses*, Oxford, Clarendon Press, 1961, p. 151.

14 I have set out some of the reasons why conservatism has ceased to be a coherent social or political philosophy in John Gray and David Willetts, *Is Conservatism Dead?*, London, Profile Books, 1997, pp. 3–65, 145–63.

15 Wittgenstein, *Philosophical Investigations*, p. 50, § 125.

16 Friedrich Nietzsche, *Joyful Wisdom*, tr. Thomas Commow, New York: Frederick Ungar, 1960, p. 160, § 116.

17 J.S. Mill, *On Liberty and Other Essays*, ed. John Gray, Oxford, Oxford University Press, 1998, p. 139.

18 For a discussion of these issues on which I cannot improve, see Isaiah Berlin, 'From Hope and Fear Set Free', in *The Proper Study of Mankind*, pp. 91–118.

19 That Berlinian value-pluralism and Millian utilitarianism are variants of ethical realism is recognized by Richard Wollheim in his interesting paper 'John Stuart Mill and Isaiah Berlin: The Ends of Life and the Preliminaries of Morality', in John Gray and G.W. Smith, eds, *J.S. Mill 'On Liberty' in Focus*, London and New York, Routledge, 1991, pp. 260–77. For an extremely interesting discussion of the relations of objectivity with will and desire, see Wollheim's 'The Sheep and the Ceremony'.

20 The irrealist view of ethics I attribute to Nietzsche is akin to that developed in the philosophy of science (and art) by Nelson Goodman. See Goodman, *Ways of Worldmaking* and *Languages of Art*. A somewhat similar view is intimated in Wittgenstein's *On Certainty*.

An excellent account of Nietzsche's perspectivism in ethics is given in Alexander Nehamas, *Nietzsche: Life as Literature*, Cambridge, Mass., and London, Harvard University Press, 1985. An illuminating account of the tensions and inconsistencies in Nietzsche's account of morality and moral knowledge may be found in Peter Berkowitz, *Nietzsche: The Ethics of an Immoralist*, Cambridge, Mass., Harvard University Press, 1995. A useful account of Nietzsche's views on truth is given by Maudemarie Clark, *Nietzsche on Truth and Philosophy*, Cambridge, Cambridge University Press, 1990.

21　I mistakenly endorsed internal realism in my *Isaiah Berlin*, pp. 72ff. Many of the issues raised by internal realism are discussed by David Wiggins in *Needs, Values, Truth*, Revised Edition, Oxford, Blackwell, 1991.

Chapter 3　Rival Freedoms

1　John Rawls, *Political Liberalism*, New York, Columbia University Press, 1993, p. 162.

2　John Rawls, *A Theory of Justice*, Oxford, Oxford University Press, 1972, pp. 124, 250, 302.

3　H.L.A. Hart, 'Rawls on Liberty and Its Priority', in *Essays in Jurisprudence and Philosophy*, Oxford, Clarendon Press, 1983, pp. 223–47.

4　Rawls, *A Theory of Justice*, p. 61.

5　Rawls, *Political Liberalism*, p. 296.

6　See Saul Kripke, *Wittgenstein on Rules and Private Language*, Oxford, Basil Blackwell, 1982, for an illuminating exposition of Wittgenstein's rule-scepticism. For the purposes of my argument it does not matter whether Kripke's interpretation of Wittgenstein is that best supported by the textual evidence.

7　For an argument that Rawls's account of the fact of pluralism itself presupposes some aspects of his own comprehensive conception of the good, see Stephen Mulhall and Adam Swift, *Liberals and Communitarians*, Second Edition, Oxford, Blackwell, 1996, pp. 231–40.

8　For an illuminating discussion of some of the difficulties of Rawls's account of pluralism, see Joseph Raz, 'Facing Diversity: The Case of Epistemic Abstinence', in his *Ethics in the Public Domain: Essays in the Morality of Law and Politics*, Oxford, Clarendon Press, 1994, pp. 45–81.

9   Rawls, *Political Liberalism*, pp. 295–7.
10 For an examination of some of the deeper difficulties of Rawls's account of the relations of the primary goods with justice, see Avishai Margalit, *The Decent Society*, Cambridge, Mass., and London, Harvard University Press, 1996, pp. 271–91. The difficulties of Rawls's theory of primary goods suggest problems for his account of practical reason, particularly his notion of a rational plan of life. For a subtle criticism of Rawls that focuses on his conception of a rational life plan, see Charles Larmore, 'The Idea of a Life Plan', *Social Philosophy and Policy*, vol. 16, no. 1, Winter 1999, pp. 96–112. Larmore argues persuasively that Rawls's conception of a rational life plan is defeated by the essential contingency of personal experience.
11 Rawls, *Political Liberalism*, p. 341.
12 For a valuable discussion of 'neutral' liberal principles, see William Galston, 'Defending Liberalism', *American Political Science Review*, no. 76, 1982, p. 662ff. A canonical critique of the use of the idea of neutrality in recent Kantian liberalism may be found in Joseph Raz, 'Neutral Political Concern', in his *The Morality of Freedom*, Oxford, Clarendon Press, 1986, pp. 110–33. See also Will Kymlicka's 'Liberal Individualism and Liberal Neutrality', *Ethics*, no. XCIX, 1989, pp. 883–905, reprinted in Shlomo Avinieri and Avner de-Shalit, eds, *Communitarianism and Individualism*, Oxford, Oxford University Press, 1992, pp. 165–85.
13 John Rawls, 'The Domain of the Political and Overlapping Consensus', in *Collected Papers*, ed. Samuel Freeman, Cambridge, Mass., and London, Harvard University Press, 1999, p. 480.
14 Isaiah Berlin, 'Introduction' to *Four Essays On Liberty*, Oxford, Oxford University Press, 1969, p. 1.
15 See Robert Nozick, *Anarchy, State and Utopia*, Oxford and New York, Basil Blackwell, 1974, pp. 30ff.
16 Ibid., p. 30, footnote.
17 J.S. Mill, *On Liberty and Other Essays*, ed. John Gray, Oxford, Oxford University Press, 1998, p. 15.
18 Ibid., pp. 13–14.
19 Mill believed that reasonable people would converge in their judgements on harm. He may have been led to this view by his views on moral epistemology. For a powerful reinterpretation of Mill's views on these questions, see John Skorupski, *John Stuart Mill*, London and New York, Routledge, 1989, chs 1, 8,

9. See also Skorupski's 'Introduction: The Fortunes of Liberal Naturalism', in John Skorupski, ed., *The Cambridge Companion to Mill*, Cambridge, Cambridge University Press, 1998, pp. 1–34.

20 I consider the difficulties of Mill's Principle of Liberty in my *Mill on Liberty: A Defence*, Second Edition, London and New York, Routledge, 1996, ch. 3 and postscript. I discussed the insuperable difficulties of a distinguished contemporary reformulation of Millian liberalism, Joel Feinberg's four-volume *The Moral Limits of the Criminal Law*, Oxford, Oxford University Press, 1984, in my *Post-liberalism: Studies in Political Thought*, London and New York, Routledge, 1993, ch. 16.

21 For Stephen's views, see *Liberty, Equality, Fraternity*, ed. Stuart D. Warner, Indianapolis, Liberty Fund, 1993.

22 See Karl Popper, *All Life is Problem-solving*, London and New York, Routledge, 1999.

23 See Ronald Dworkin, *Taking Rights Seriously*, New York, Basic Books, 1983, ch. 12, and *A Matter of Principle*, Oxford, Oxford University Press, 1985.

24 Rawls, 'Reply to Alexander and Musgrave', in *Collected Papers*, p. 238.

25 See Michael Walzer, *Spheres of Justice*, New York, Basic Books, 1983. For a development of Walzer's views, see his *Thick and Thin: Moral Argument at Home and Abroad*, Notre Dame, Ind., and London, Notre Dame Press, 1994, and *On Toleration*, New Haven, Conn., and London, Yale University Press, 1997.

26 Isaiah Berlin, 'Two Concepts of Liberty', in *The Proper Study of Mankind*, ed. Henry Hardy and Roger Hausheer, London, Chatto and Windus, 1997, p. 202.

27 For a criticism of Berlin's account of negative liberty that is (in some respects) parallel with my own, see Charles Taylor, 'What's Wrong with Negative Liberty', in David Miller, ed., *Liberty*, Oxford, Oxford University Press, 1991, pp. 141–62. Taylor's *Sources of the Self: The Making of the Modern Identity*, Cambridge, Cambridge University Press, 1989, contains much that is germane to these questions.

28 Berlin, 'Two Concepts of Liberty', p.197. An illuminating discussion of Berlin's views on this point may be found in Sydney Morganbesser and Jonathan Lieberson, 'Isaiah Berlin', in Edna and Avishai Margalit, eds, *Isaiah Berlin: A Celebration*, London, The Hogarth Press, 1991, pp. 1–30.

29 Joseph Raz, 'Facing Up: A Reply', *Southern California Law*

Review, vol. 62, nos. 3 and 4, March–May 1989, p. 1227.

30 Raz, *The Morality of Freedom*, pp. 369–70.

31 See Bhikhu Parekh, 'Superior People: The Narrowness of Liberalism from Rawls to Mill', *Times Literary Supplement*, 25 February 1994.

32 In later writings, Raz has defended a liberal version of multiculturalism. See Joseph Raz, *Ethics in the Public Domain: Essays in the Morality of Law and Politics*, Oxford, Clarendon Press, 1994, ch. 7. In *The Morality of Freedom*, Raz's argument for the value of autonomy is partly an argument for assimilation to a liberal majority. It is not clear how much force Raz thinks this contextual argument for the value of autonomy has in highly multicultural societies. In societies where there is no majority culture – still less a liberal majority – adopting liberal values cannot be a condition of personal well-being. Like many other liberal thinkers, Raz takes for granted that the animating morality of multicultural societies is bound to be liberal.

33 Raz, *The Morality of Freedom*, p. 370.

34 Ibid., p. 369.

35 Raz, *Ethics in the Public Domain*, pp. 103–4.

36 For an argument that value-pluralism does not mean that particular settlements of conflicts of value cannot be rationally justified, see Berys Gaut, 'Rag-bags, Disputes and Moral Pluralism', *Utilitas*, vol. 11, no. 1, March 1999, pp. 37–48.

Chapter 4 *Modus Vivendi*

1 For Hume's incisive argument against the precursors of contemporary liberalism, see David Hume, 'Of the Original Contract', in *Essays, Moral, Political and Literary*, Indianapolis, Liberty Fund, 1984.

2 I have considered some of the confusions surrounding moral relativism and liberal universalism in international contexts in 'Global Utopias and Clashing Civilizations: Misunderstanding the Present', *International Relations*, vol. 74, no. 1, January 1998, pp. 149–63.

3 See Bernard Lewis, *The Middle East*, London, Weidenfeld and Nicolson, 1995, pp. 321–3:

> A *millet* was a religio-political community defined by its adherence to a religion. Its members were subject to the rules and even to the laws of that religion, administered by its own chiefs.

... In return for this measure of religious freedom and communal autonomy, non-Muslim *millets* owed allegiance to the state ... ethnic solidarities did not define basic identity, nor did they determine ultimate allegiance. The people whom we call, and who now call themselves, Turks and Arabs, did not describe themselves by these names until fairly modern times.
... It was only in modern times, under the impact of European ideas of nationality, that literate city-dwellers began to describe themselves by these ethnic terms.

4   See Avishai Margalit's book *The Decent Society*, Cambridge, Mass., and London, Harvard University Press, 1996, for an excellent examination of the moral significance of humiliation.

5   I have examined, and rejected, the common distinctions between negative rights and welfare rights in a more extended and systematic fashion in my *Beyond the New Right: Markets, Government and the Common Environment*, London and New York, Routledge, 1993, pp. 99–110.

6   *The Universal Declaration of Human Rights*, London, Waterstone's and the Medical Foundation for the Care of Victims of Torture, 1998.

7   Benedict de Spinoza, *A Theologico-Political Treatise*, tr. R.H.M. Elwes, New York, Dover Publications, 1951, p. 245. An illuminating account of Spinoza's views on freedom of religion may be found in Stuart Hampshire, *Spinoza*, Harmondsworth, Penguin Books, 1951, ch. 5.

8   The account of rights I have sketched is broadly in line with that advanced by Joseph Raz in his *The Morality of Freedom*, Oxford, Clarendon Press, 1986, chs 7, 8 and 10. It may be worth noting that there is nothing in the logic of rights which implies that they can be held only by humans.

9   For an examination of the ways in which population density can diminish liberty, see Jack Parsons, *Population versus Liberty*, London, Pemberton Books, 1971.

10 Neil Belton, *The Good Listener: Helen Bamber – A Life Against Cruelty*, London, Weidenfeld and Nicolson, 1998, p. 322.

11 A powerful statement of the communitarian critique of liberalism can be found in Michael Sandel, *Liberalism and the Limits of Justice*, Cambridge, Cambridge University Press, 1982. For a brilliant discussion of the issues raised by communitarian and perfectionist conceptions of government, see William A. Galston, *Liberal Purposes: Goods, Virtues and Diversity in the Liberal State*, Cambridge, Cambridge University Press, 1991.

12 For critiques of communitarianism, see my *Liberalisms: Essays in Political Philosophy*, London and New York, Routledge, 1989, pp. 233ff.; *Post-liberalism: Studies in Political Thought*, London and New York, Routledge, 1993, pp. 261ff.; and chs 1, 8 and 9 in my *Enlightenment's Wake: Politics and Culture at the Close of the Modern Age*, London and New York, Routledge, 1995.

13 I owe the term 'Counter-Enlightenment' to Isaiah Berlin, whose use of it I discuss in my *Isaiah Berlin*, London and Princeton, NJ, HarperCollins and Princeton University Press, 1995, ch. 5. Berlin's use of the term is explained in 'The Counter-Enlightenment', in his *The Proper Study of Mankind*, ed. Henry Hardy and Roger Hausheer, London, Chatto and Windus, 1997, pp. 243–68. See also Berlin's 'The First Attack on Enlightenment', in his *The Roots of Romanticism*, ed. Henry Hardy, London, Chatto and Windus, 1999, pp. 21–45.

14 For an attempt to map the dialectic of the self-undermining of the Enlightenment and an analysis of fundamentalism as an attempt at the re-enchantment of the world, see my *Enlightenment's Wake*, ch. 10. See also my *Voltaire and Enlightenment*, London, Phoenix, 1998.

15 Lord Acton and F.A. Hayek are among liberal thinkers who criticized the commitment of classical liberalism to the nation-state. But they failed to understand the needs that the nation-state served, and their writings on the subject are accordingly dry and utopian.

16 For an examination of the complexities of nationalism, see Tom Nairn, *Faces of Nationalism: Janus Revisited*, London, Verso, 1998.

17 'Mother Tongue Divides France', *The Independent* (London), 28 June 1999.

18 On the decline of Clausewitzian armed conflict, see Martin van Creveld's brilliant study *Future War*, London, Brassey, 1991.

19 I do not mean that the argument that democracies must be small is all that there is to republican theory. A key contention of 'neo-Roman' political thinkers was that force and coercion are not the only, nor always the most important, constraints on individual liberty. For an illuminating account of these neo-Roman thinkers and their relations with liberalism, see Quentin Skinner's excellent *Liberty Before Liberalism*, Cambridge, Cambridge University Press, 1998.

20 For an intriguing revisionist interpretation of American federalism, presented in the context of a re-evaluation of the

philosophy of David Hume, see Donald W. Livingstone, *Philo-sophical Melancholy and Delirium: Hume's Pathology of Philoso-phy*, Chicago, University of Chicago Press, 1998.

21 For an illuminating account of the diplomatic and military op-erations surrounding cross-border enforcement of human rights, see Gwyn Prins, *European Horizons of Diplomatic/Military Op-erations*, London, The Royal Institute of International Affairs (International Security Programme), 1999.

22 For a fascinating survey of the causes and consequences of cor-roded and collapsed states, see Manuel Castells, *End of Millen-nium*, Oxford, Blackwell, 1998.

23 Thomas Hobbes, *Leviathan*, Oxford, Oxford University Press, 1996, p. 85.

24 In contemporary circumstances, environmental conservation is a precondition of anything resembling commodious living. Yet in the absence of an effective modern state – that is to say, in much of the world – environmental conservation is impos-sible.

25 Elias Canetti has some interesting observations on the unreal-ity of Hobbes's individualist account of the war of all against all in *Crowds and Power*, London, Picador, 1986, pp. 115ff.

26 In prizing fidelity to ethical and political life over theoretical consistency, the neo-Hobbesian view I have sketched resem-bles the agonistic liberalism I have attributed to Isaiah Berlin. See my *Isaiah Berlin*, ch. 6.

27 Friedrich Nietzsche, *On the Genealogy of Morality*, tr. Maudemarie Clark and Alan J. Swensen, Indianapolis and Cam-bridge, Hackett Publishing Co., 1998, pp. 107–11. For a pen-etrating interpretation of Nietzsche's views on truth, illusion and value, see Alexander Nehemas, *Nietzsche: Life as Litera-ture*, Cambridge, Mass., and London, Harvard University Press, 1985.

28 The liberal philosophies criticized in earlier works of mine are all of them Enlightenment universalist liberalisms. The post-liberal standpoint I have defended is one that seeks to over-come the limitations of those liberalisms. See my 'What is Dead and What is Living in Liberalism' in *Post-liberalism*, pp. 283–328; 'From Post-liberalism to Pluralism', in *Enlightenment's Wake*, pp. 131–43; 'Where Pluralists and Liberals Part Com-pany', *International Journal of Philosophical Studies*, vol. 6, no. 1, 1998, pp. 17–36, and 'Mill's Liberalism and Liberalism's Posterity', *Journal of Ethics*, Winter, 1999.

Index